INSIDE OUT

___

SEX AND POWER
AT THE
BEAU RIVAGE

___

NEW WELSH DRAMA III

INSIDE OUT

Leslie Ross

in collaboration with

Chris Morgan

SEX AND POWER AT THE BEAU RIVAGE

Lewis Davies

NEW WELSH DRAMA III

PARTHIAN

Parthian
The Old Surgery
Napier Street
Cardigan
SA43 1ED

www.parthianbooks.co.uk

First published in 2006
© The authors 2006
All Rights Reserved

ISBN 1 902638 35 2
     9 781902 638355

Cover design by Lucy Llewllyn
Inner design by www.lloydrobson.com
Printed and bound by Dinefwr Press, Llandybïe, Wales

Published with the financial support of the Welsh
Books Council

British Library Cataloguing in Publication Data – A
cataloguing record for this book is available from the
British Library

Production enquiries for *Inside Out* to Peters Fraser and
Dunlop Group Ltd. All Rights Reserved

CONTENTS

Introduction   vii
Chris Morgan

Inside Out   1
Lesley Ross in collaboration with Chris Morgan

Sex and Power at the Beau Rivage   107
Lewis Davies

INTRODUCTION

Two Welshmen who came to prominence in the first half of the twentieth century. As young men they both left Wales to pursue their careers in London.

Ivor Novello was the archetypal matinee idol, making a major contribution to the history of musical theatre. His name lives on in the prestigious Ivor Novello Music Awards.

Rhys Davies was a prolific short story writer and novelist, who was awarded the OBE for services to literature in 1968. In Wales there is a biennial Rhys Davies Short Story Competition.

Both men were gay at a time when homosexuality was still illegal. Novello lived at the heart of the West End's social scene, and Davies was at the fringe of the Bloomsbury Group, but in the wider world, inevitably very little was known about their private lives.

Although it is not clear if the two men knew each other, Rhys Davies used Novello as the inspiration for the central character in one of his most popular novels, *The Painted King*.

The two plays here, do not attempt to tell the whole biographical story, rather they look at turning points in each of the men's lives.

Inside Out is inspired by Novello's own diary entries written during the time of his imprisonment at Wormwood Scrubs, *Sex and Power at the Beau Rivage* is based on Rhys Davies's description of his meeting with Frieda and D H Lawrence at Bandol on the Cote D'Azur in the late 1920's.

The publication of these plays will hopefully remind people of the significant contribution made by both men – Rhys Davies in the field of literature and Ivor Novello in the world of theatre and music.

Chris Morgan, Artistic Director, Theatr Y Byd

LESLEY ROSS

Lesley Ross studied Psychology at Nottingham University before training as an actor at the Welsh College of Music and Drama.

He has worked extensively in both adult and children's theatre as actor, writer and director. In 1992, he set up Ripley Theatre and every year for a decade he produced a new show at the Edinburgh Fringe, including three Fringe First Nominees.

Other plays include *The Little Tempest* (National Theatre), *The Gorgeous Lives of Seahorses* (Made In Wales), *My Brother's Conversion* (Royal Welsh College of Music and Drama), *Love & Other Ambiguities* (Theatr Y Byd) and *Shared Mutual Experience* (Sherman/HTV Wales).

As a lyricist he has written the book and lyrics for *Gold Woman* (Unknown Theatre), *The Jolly Folly of Polly The Scottish Trolley Dolly* (Ripley Theatre), and for the children's musicals *Jorinda & Jorindel* (WNO), *Rumpelstiltskin* (Cardiff Everyman), and the six shows that make up *The Sheep Chronicles*.

His *International Festival of Lilliput* premiered in Hong Kong (2002).

CHRIS MORGAN

Chris Morgan was born in Cardiff and trained as an actor at the Royal Welsh College of Music and Drama. He has been Artistic Director of Theatr Y Byd since 2001. Recent productions include the award-winning *Flowers from Tunisia* by Laurence Allan and *Butterfly* by Ian Rowlands.

For five years he was Associate Director of Hijinx Theatre, working alongside writers on the development of five new plays. He has written biographical shows based on the lives of both Doris Day and Richard Burton. He is collaborating with James Williams on a new muscial version of *The Picture of Dorian Gray*. He continues to work as a freelance actor and director.

INSIDE OUT
A PORTRAIT OF IVOR NOVELLO

For Patricia Hochron – always with me

LESLEY ROSS
IN COLLABORATION WITH
CHRIS MORGAN

Inside Out – A Portrait of Ivor Novello was first produced by Theatr Y Byd at the Torch Theatre, Milford Haven, on Thursday 27th September 2001.

Cast:

Ivor Novello	–	Roland Powell
Leading Lady/Fan	–	Helen Evans
Olive/Mam	–	Nina Holloway
Bobbie Andrews	–	Ceris Jones
Chorus Boy/Padre	–	Dyfed Potter

The parts of the Leading Lady and the Fan should always be played by the same actor.

Creative Team:

Director	–	Chris Morgan
Designer	–	Sean Crowley
Production Manager	–	David Roxburgh

Featuring songs and dialogue
from Ivor Novello's *The Dancing Years*.

ACT ONE
Scene One

Dressing Room – somewhere in England.

Early 1942 – The Dancing Years *is on tour. Part of* The Dancing Years *overture plays. A CHORUS BOY in his early twenties is stood in Ivor's dressing room. He is wearing a coat and has a small suitcase at his feet. He faces upstage. BOBBIE enters.*

BOBBIE: Hello.

BOY: Hello. Um...

BOBBIE: And you are?

BOY: I'm Edward.

BOBBIE: Olive, come quickly. There's something you should see.

OLIVE (*entering and looking at the BOY*): What is it?

BOBBIE: I'm not sure. This is Edward.

OLIVE: Hello Edward.

BOY: I was sent up from London.

BOBBIE: Really? Olive, it's not Christmas already, is it?.

OLIVE: No, it isn't.

BOBBIE: Shame.

OLIVE: Edward what?

BOY: Um, Edward...

BOBBIE: Edward Edward? How delightful.

BOY: No, Edward French. I was told to come in and wait for Mr Novello. I'm replacing someone.

BOBBIE: Ah, so our dear Mr X will be seen no more. He has mysteriously disappeared and immediately he is replaced with Mr W. Let's hope you come up to scratch, Edward French. Ivor fires people so discreetly. Who could be next?

BOY: Actually, it's Eddie.

OLIVE: Well, Eddie, don't listen to a word he says, no one has been fired. We've just lost another actor to the war effort. Welcome to the tour.

BOBBIE: It's not quite the war, but it has its moments.

OLIVE: Don't worry about him, dear. I'm Olive Gilbert.

BOY: I know, I saw you in London. You were very good as the singing teacher.

OLIVE smiles.

BOBBIE: You haven't seen me play the part.

OLIVE: Bobbie, leave the boy alone. This dear creature is Robert Andrews.

BOBBIE (*smiles*): Actually it's Bobbie. So, are you a big fan?

BOY: Oh, yes, I've seen three of his shows, now.

BOBBIE (*to OLIVE*): I was talking about me, wasn't I?

OLIVE: Don't be so beastly. So, who sent you in here, exactly?

LADY (*entering*): I did. Isn't he adorable? And he's called Eddie, like Eddie Marsh, Ivor will be thrilled.

BOBBIE: I'm sure.

LADY: Now, I hope you haven't been completely awful to the boy. They haven't been teasing you, awfully, have they?

BOY: No, not at all.

LADY: I've already admonished him, haven't I? Of all the songs in the show he likes *My Life Belongs To You*. The duet. Well, tonight you are only to watch me, I insist on it. You mustn't give the tenor a second glance, but keep your eyes fixed firmly on me. Where is Ivor?

OLIVE: Signing autographs?

LADY: Typical. Now, whatever you do, don't be nervous, just be yourself. Do you know, Eddie here saw us at the Lane, and now he's with us on tour. Isn't that a most lovely coincidence?

Beat.

OLIVE: Mmm. Yes. Well it's lovely that you are here.

BOBBIE: I'll tell you another interesting little coincidence, Eddie, which refers specifically to your name. Or rather to Edward Marsh's name. It was during the run of *Careless Rapture*...

IVOR appears at the door.

BOBBIE: And Eddie and I had taken a dislike to a rather tiresome usherette who insisted on...

IVOR (*entering*): Oh Bobbie, please. Not again! I'm sure there's plenty of time to acquaint yourself with the dear boy, but must we hear that story once again.

OLIVE: I second that.

BOBBIE: It is a very amusing story.

LADY: Not when it's the twelfth time you've heard it.

IVOR: Only twelve? Darling, where've you been?

BOBBIE: You are all evil personified, and I wish nothing more to do with you.

IVOR: As you wish, Duckie. Now, it's Edward, isn't it?

BOY: Eddie.

IVOR: Well of course it is.

LADY: I found him loitering at the stage door.

BOY: I managed to get an earlier train than expected.

IVOR: Why that's marvellous. Welcome to the tour. A new breath to give the old donkey a little life.

LADY: Oh, Ivor, he'll be wonderful. He danced the leap year waltz for a charity gala.

IVOR: How divine. You've acquainted yourself with our lovely leading lady, then, I see.

BOY: She was extremely helpful when I arrived. I'm indebted to you.

LADY: Not at all, darling. My pleasure.

IVOR: Well, isn't this heaven? A new addition to the tour. Can there be anything more enjoyable than this? Than this job we do? How perfectly frightful to be anyone else?

BOBBIE: You mean not having to travel though the blackouts.

OLIVE: Or sleep in a church hall.

BOBBIE: Eat the local delicacies.

LADY: Oh, it's all so glamorous.

IVOR: Ignore them all, dear boy, nothing can compare to the hustle and bustle of a tour. Why, every new town provides us with a glittering first night. It's like a continuous house party. And that's with a nice little cheque at the end of every week, too.

OLIVE: We do like the cheque, it must be said.

IVOR: Touring is an absolute delight.

BOY: I drink to that, Mr Novello.

IVOR: It's Ivor, dear boy. No one calls me Mr Novello except a few misguided theatre critics. Always Ivor.

The BOY nods.

IVOR: Now, you'll watch this evening, and then tomorrow we'll get you fitted into costume.

BOY: That would be marvellous, thank you.

IVOR: You can watch with Mr Andrews, seeing as I didn't write a part for him.

BOBBIE: I declined the one offered, as a matter of fact, Mr Novello.

OLIVE: Yes, Bobbie, of course. Now, I think it time we left you to prepare. I believe we have a show to do. (*She exits.*)

IVOR: Yes, indeed, darling. Time to lift the morale once more.

LADY: And remember your promise. (*She exits.*)

IVOR: I do hope you enjoy it, dear boy. It has changed somewhat since we were at the Lane.

BOBBIE: Oh, I'm sure he'll enjoy it as much as I will. Shall we?

IVOR: Yes, off you go. Once more unto the breach, dear friends, once more!

The BOY stops.

IVOR: What is it dear boy?

BOY: Well, I saw you play Henry, as a matter of fact.

BOBBIE coughs.

IVOR: Don't say a word, Mr Andrews. Did you enjoy it?

BOY: Yes, but not as much as I will tonight. I desperately want to be on the stage with you all.

IVOR: Well dear boy, this is just the start. (*Looking into the mirror.*) You know, we live a charmed life in the theatre. We're somehow lucky enough to avoid all the ugliness, don't you think?

BOY: I couldn't agree more.

BOBBIE: Yes, indeed, but one mustn't keep your fans waiting, Mr Novello.

IVOR: Bobbie, please don't be a bore. And do look after the boy properly, will you. Make sure you bring him back after the show. (*To the BOY:*) M has acquired a rather delightful restaurateur who is taking some of the gang for dinner. I do hope you'll be able to join us?

BOY: Well, yes of course. I'd like that very much.

IVOR: Besides, I've got some big news for everyone, and I'd quite like to announce it this very evening.

BOBBIE: I'm sure that can wait until later, can't it?

IVOR: Nonsense, Eddie here can keep a little secret, I'm sure. Can I trust you to be discreet, Eddie? Until I make my announcement?

BOY: Of course.

IVOR: Well then, *The Dancing Years* is going back to London.

BOY: To the Lane?

IVOR: No dear boy, to The Adelphi. It's exactly the news everyone has been hoping for. And so life will be wonderful all over again. Isn't that right, Mr Andrews?

BOBBIE: If you say so.

IVOR: Well, then, take our new recruit into battle.

BOBBIE: Yes. Yes of course.

Beat.

BOBBIE: Follow me.

They exit. There is music as the light fades on the dressing room, and IVOR enters the world of The Dancing Years.

Interlude A – A Scene from *The Dancing Years*

LADY: The bullies are getting stronger everyday – turning our whole world upside down.

The light comes up on IVOR, as Rudi.

IVOR: All the more reason for me to carry on resisting them. I don't mind the danger. Even when they locked me up, I didn't mind – my thoughts were far away, somewhere with you – back over the years. *The Dancing Years* – some happy, some sad, but all so full of wonderful memories.

LADY: For both of us. They'll come again. And you know what they will say. You made the whole world dance.

Music is heard as the lights fade on IVOR.

Interlude B – Another Scene from *The Dancing Years*, Later in the Tour

A Spotlight on the LEADING LADY. Although this is a duet, we only hear her part.

LADY (*sings* My Life Belongs to You):
    'My life belongs to you
    My dreams, my songs, all that I do
    No moon, no morning star can shine
    No happiness is mine
    Without you near me
    When years have passed into the shade
    You'll hear my last serenade
    Forever echoing anew;
    No matter where you go
    Your listening heart will know
    My life belongs to you.'

Applause is heard and the lights fade on The Dancing Years *and return to dressing room.*

Scene Two

Ivor's dressing room, somewhere on tour.

Early 1942 – The Dancing Years *on tour. This scene happens a few weeks after Scene One. IVOR and BOBBIE have glasses of champagne. There is the sound of laughter.*

IVOR: What on earth?

The BOY rushes into the dressing room, followed by OLIVE.

BOY: Gentlemen, you have just missed the most hysterical event. Barry's been teaching M Olive's part for The Wings of Sleep.

BOBBIE: And was he singing M's part?

OLIVE: Of Course.

BOY: You must come, Mr Ivor. No disrespect to your music, but it's hysterically funny. He's now teaching her to sing Uniform. (*To BOBBIE:*) You should see the look on M's face.

OLIVE: He is rather taking her to task.

IVOR: Stop and have a drink, darlings. Olive, what would you like?

OLIVE: What I would like is to go back to London. But failing that, I'll settle for a glass of champagne.

IVOR: For you, darling, anything.

BOBBIE gets her a drink.

IVOR: And we will be home soon.

OLIVE: Oh keep telling me that. Four weeks to London. I can hardly wait.

IVOR: You're just miffed that your part isn't bigger.

OLIVE: That's unfair. (*To the BOY:*) I had much more to do in Careless Rapture. (*To IVOR:*) You could write me a little solo in Uniform, couldn't you? Surround me with a group of these young soldiers and let me sing to them.

IVOR: What a delightful idea.

BOY: We'd be more than happy to let you join our ranks.

IVOR: Ah, yes, but what would you wear, darling?

OLIVE: I think I should look rather fetching in Eddie's uniform, actually.

IVOR: But of course.

BOY: It certainly looks very appealing on M.

IVOR: M's wearing your costume? How marvellous.

OLIVE: It's not that marvellous. (*To BOBBIE:*) Pour me another, darling.

IVOR: Later, children. First, I think I should like to have a little fun with our newfound singing teacher.

BOBBIE: Barry might even like to teach *you* something from the show.

IVOR: Enough, now Bobbie.

FAN (*entering*): Oh, I think it would be wonderful if you sang in one of your shows, Mr Novello.

IVOR: My dear, I didn't realise you were there. Everyone, this charming young lady has seen *The Dancing Years* more times than even she can remember. She obviously hasn't heard me sing, but she must hold some sort of attendance record.

FAN: Oh, but I love your musicals, they are worth seeing over and over again. I still laugh and cry in all the same places, too.

IVOR: Miss Walton, you could teach Bobbie a thing or two about devotion.

BOBBIE: I'm sure.

FAN: It's really nothing, Mr Novello.

IVOR: Ivor, dear, always Ivor.

FAN: It's really nothing Mr Ivor. I don't mind coming to see you. And my work allows. We're a big commercial concern, now, and I'm working with the Managing Director, so I just arrange meetings to coincide with your tour schedule.

BOBBIE: How dreary for you.

OLIVE giggles.

FAN: Well, only when work permits, of course, but it seems worth it.

OLIVE: Oh, I think it's very sweet of you, dear. Ivor is worth it, after all.

FAN: I couldn't agree more, Miss Gilbert.

OLIVE (*glancing over at BOBBIE*): Grace, isn't it?

FAN: Yes that's right, Grace Walton. Well, it's my middle name.

IVOR: Well, Grace, it's people like you who make the touring bearable for this wretched lot. Where would they be without you, my dear devoted fans?

BOBBIE (*to OLIVE*): In London.

OLIVE laughs.

FAN: Where would we be without you, Mr Ivor?

IVOR: Possibly following someone else around the country?

BOBBIE (*to OLIVE*): Like Mr Coward.

IVOR: Bobbie, enough. Will we see you tomorrow night, Miss Walton?

FAN: Yes of course, Mr Ivor. I don't return home till Monday.

IVOR: Marvellous. And now, a singing lesson awaits us. Come along.

They exit. The FAN returns for a second, examining the room.

FAN: Four weeks to London. (*She scurries off.*)

Music plays. Time passes.

Scene Three

Ivor's dressing room, The Adelphi.

Christmas Eve, 1942.

IVOR (*enters, examining a scarf that OLIVE has bought him*): It's marvellous, Olive, I adore it. How I love Christmas in London. You don't mind that I opened it early, do you? Can I wear it now, this evening? Olive?

OLIVE (*following, but looking out*): Oh, I'm sorry Ivor, what did you say? That woman is here again.

IVOR: Where?

OLIVE: At the Stage Door.

IVOR: Did she see the show again? Doesn't she have a home to go to, it's Christmas Eve? Tell them to let her in, dear, let's give her a little Christmas treat. A glass of champagne with the cast, eh?

OLIVE: Yes, but don't you even think about inviting her back.

IVOR: Are you drunk? I wouldn't dream of it. Ruin a perfectly good fan. Where would I be, then? But one does have to rely on one's public for one's sense of self-esteem, and she does play the fawning fan so well. I think I should be more concerned if she wasn't there.

OLIVE: But she's such a complete nuisance. And she's a dreadful bore.

IVOR: Oh, I know, darling. She is a bore. What a bore. What an awful bore. But what a dear, she is. What an absolute dear. Surely you can suffer her for a few moments?

OLIVE: And Bobbie? He'll be here soon.

IVOR: Bobbie can go hang! It's a few minutes grace for what is, probably, my biggest fan. And I must respect my fans, mustn't I? And it is Christmas, darling, please humour me.

Beat.

IVOR (*he lifts her present.*): I simply adore this.

OLIVE: Ivor, you're far too soft, but as it's Christmas, I'll let her in.

OLIVE exits and IVOR pours himself a drink.

IVOR (*humming or singing*): 'O come all ye faithful
                    Joyful and triumphant
                    O come ye, o come ye
                    To Bethlehem.'
      Now, that's a money-spinner.

OLIVE enters with the FAN.

OLIVE: Come in, come in.

IVOR: Yes, do come in, have a glass of champagne. Or sherry.

FAN: Well, if you're sure. A sherry, thank you.

IVOR: Of course I'm sure, dear, it Christmas.

FAN: And you were especially good tonight. I think *The Dancing Years* will be my all time favourite.

IVOR: Until the next one, I hope.

FAN: No, I'm sure this will be my favourite. That scene when you discover you have a little son. It's so sad. (*Takes sherry from OLIVE.*) Thank you. Well, not sad, tragic.

IVOR: Not too sentimental, I hope?

FAN: What's wrong with that? We need things to take us away from this dreadful war. I believe that you've done more for the war effort than anyone else, Mr Ivor.

IVOR: Well, one does one's best.

FAN: Oh you do much, much more than that. You keep up morale, Mr Ivor. My Uncle fought in The Great War and he was singing *Keep The Home Fires Burning* when they entered Palestine. They all were. So you have done so much for so many in both wars. Yes. And I would punch any one on the nose who said you didn't.

IVOR: Maybe we should send you out to war, Miss Walton.

OLIVE: Ivor, haven't we got to get ready for Bobbie?

IVOR: Excuse me, we're winning the War here, aren't we, Miss Walton?

FAN: Oh yes, Mr Ivor, if you say so.

IVOR: Do you know, when we first sang that song...

OLIVE: Which is officially called...

IVOR (*cutting her off*): Thank you, Olive. Well, you see I played and this lovely woman called Sybil Vane sang, and do you know, they had learnt the chorus after a single hearing. They all joined in the second refrain. It's true, isn't it, Olive?

OLIVE: They had to sing it about nine times.

IVOR: And where did it lead us? Here we are drinking Sherry at the Adelphi Theatre. (*To OLIVE:*) Not quite the Lane, but then I can't imagine anywhere else now.

OLIVE puts on a smile.

FAN: That's the beauty of *The Dancing Years*, Mr Ivor, it would work anywhere. And I think, despite this awful war, this could be the best Christmas I've ever had. When your Henry V closed I was so worried you wouldn't write something soon, and then you wrote *The Dancing Years* and that terrible waiting was over. That awful waiting, sitting at home singing your songs, speaking your lines – I never really got on with Shakespeare, and after all, it wasn't your words, so it doesn't really count, but your words, I know them all, Mr Ivor, all of them.

OLIVE: I wish I knew them all. Did you hear me in the first act? I was completely at sea.

FAN: Oh, I don't think anyone noticed, Miss Gilbert, and you covered it very well.

Beat.

OLIVE: Yes, well someone obviously did notice, then.

FAN: Oh, I don't count; I'm not seeing it for the first time.

IVOR (*winks at OLIVE*): But surely you don't know all the words, Miss Walton?

FAN: Maria, there's not much time and I have so many things to say. I love you and only you. You have always been the colour and the magic in my life and nothing can ever take that away.

IVOR: Why, that's marvellous.

FAN: No, wait, this is my favourite part...

OLIVE rolls her eyes.

FAN: There is so much unrest and unhappiness in the world. We are going to see great changes. We will almost forget to smile and make music, but not quite. I know, I feel it. One day, we'll wake as if from an evil dream and forget to hate, and the world will smile again...

BOBBIE enters.

FAN: And music and friendship will... oh, I'm sorry.

BOBBIE: Well, Mr Novello, you seem to have been usurped. Finish it please.

FAN: Oh, I'd feel silly and I'm getting light headed anyway, so I really ought to go now. Have a very Merry Christmas Mr Ivor.

IVOR: Please, no, finish your drink, at least.

OLIVE: It's the rules of the dressing room. After show drinks must be finished.

FAN: Thank you. Thank you so, so much. (*She stands in the background.*)

BOBBIE (*holding up a piece of paper*): Well, it's official, Mr Novello, you can't use the car. The Ministry of War Transport considers that the railway facilities are adequate for your needs, but they might be prepared to consider the granting of a limited facility between Maidenhead and Littlewick Green – That's a whole four miles – if, and only if, you can make a strong enough case.

OLIVE: What is he talking about?

IVOR: They've turned my petrol application down. It's a bloody cheek, that's what it is. I simply want to drive down to Redroofs, my home, which I paid for with my well-earned money, just a couple of weekends every month. The railways indeed. It's outrageous!

BOBBIE (*glancing at the FAN*): Calm down, Ivor.

IVOR: No, I will not calm down. I have toured all through this war, performed during air raids and through great hardship, and now they won't even give me a little petrol? It's appalling. (*Points at the FAN.*) They were singing *Home Fires* when they marched into Palestine!

BOBBIE: Ivor, we can still...

IVOR: No, Bobbie, bugger them. Just a little petrol so that I, who am doing quite important work really, when you consider it, can recuperate and keep myself fit. I mean ENSA was set up to entertain the troops and I'm sure they're getting plenty of this marvellous petrol when they want it, but we somehow are doing something less worthy, is that it?

BOBBIE: Not now, Mr Novello.

IVOR: Don't talk to me like I'm a child, Bobbie, it's infuriating. Four miles, indeed. What an insult. Right, if that's how they want it, then fine, I don't even want the car. I'll give it away. It's not going to be much good to me doing four miles a week, is it? I'll give it to the Red Cross, I'll give it to ENSA, I'll give it to anyone who can bloody well use it!

BOBBIE: Finished?

IVOR: Well it just seems so unfair.

OLIVE: We are at war, Ivor.

IVOR: Don't you start. I need the country air, that's all. How I adore the fresh air.

Beat.

IVOR: What a Christmas present.

Beat.

IVOR: Oh well, we'll just have to give it away. (*He sits and sulks.*)

BOBBIE (*to OLIVE*): He'll be fine tomorrow. I'll see to it.

FAN (*coming forward*): Mr Ivor?

IVOR: I'm so sorry, dear, how awful of me. I do hope you have a very merry Christmas.

FAN: No it's not that, it's the car. I was just thinking. Part of my work takes me all over the country and well, if you wanted to put the car to some use.

IVOR: Yes?

FAN: Well, my firm could use it. We do a lot of work for the war effort and the car would be a great asset, and I could see that it gets taken over.

BOBBIE: Thank you, but it all sounds like far too much trouble.

FAN: Oh, I didn't mean to speak out of turn.

IVOR: No wait, wait a moment. I think it might be of great benefit to Miss Walton's firm. Why not look into it, dear. In the meantime, I have a party to go to. Olive, champagne beckons. See Miss Walton out, Mr Andrews.

IVOR and OLIVE exit.

BOBBIE: Do you have far to go?

FAN: No, it's just a short walk.

BOBBIE: Mmm.

FAN: They've been terribly unfair to him. After all, he must look after his health. Of course what he really needs is a wife.

BOBBIE: Are you not married, Miss Walton?

FAN: I was engaged once, but he didn't care too much for the theatre.

BOBBIE: Of course.

FAN: Yes. I write myself too, you know.

BOBBIE: Really, that's marvellous? Shall we go?

FAN: I even had a play produced once. But it was nothing. Not compared to him. I know all his lines. More than I know my own.

BOBBIE: Yes, I must apologise for so rudely interrupting you.

FAN: I'd nearly finished. I only had one line left.

BOBBIE: Yes. Shall we?

FAN: 'Keep me in your heart as I will keep you in mine. I won't even be unhappy now I know we have something to share.' It's a lovely line don't you think, talking about the little boy. It always makes me cry.

BOBBIE: Mmm. Shall we? (*He ushers her out.*)

Scene Four

Ivor's dressing room, The Adelphi.

1943. Music plays as the CHORUS BOY enters Ivor's dressing room. He sits, nervously. He is only half dressed.

IVOR (*entering*): My dear boy, what are you doing in here?

BOY: I'm so sorry, Mr Ivor, I didn't know who else to come to.

IVOR: What is it? Has something happened to you? You know you can tell me anything.

BOY: I feel I've been very stupid.

IVOR: Oh? What exactly have you done?

BOY: Well, I don't know how to say this.

IVOR: You'd best say it soon, hadn't you? Otherwise you'll never get back into your costume in time. I don't feel the number 'Uniform' will really work unless you're wearing one.

BOY: I'm sorry, I'm just in a bit of a panic.

IVOR: And the cause of your panic?

BOY: It's Jenny, Mr Ivor, in the chorus. I'm afraid she's...

IVOR: You haven't done anything foolish, have you?

BOY: Oh, no, nothing like that...

IVOR: Thank heavens.

BOY: It's more... she's drunk. I think. Blind drunk.

Beat.

IVOR: Drunk?

BOY: Yes, I took her for a picnic after the show this afternoon. Just to St James' Park. But she's rather not used to the alcohol, I fear, and now she's in the lavatory sitting or sleeping or something and I'm afraid I'm in for an awful row. That is, I...

IVOR: And why, then, have you come to me?

BOY: Because if I'm going to have a row, I'd rather it came from you.

IVOR: Yes, well you know what I think about alcohol, don't you?

BOY: No, not really.

IVOR: I adore it. I think it's marvellous stuff. Every good home should have at least one bottle of champagne in every room. (*He smiles.*)

Beat.

BOY: Then you're not angry?

IVOR: Dearest boy, I'm furious. These people have paid good money, some of them more than they can afford, in order to see the best show that we can possibly provide. It is therefore despicable to ever put yourself in a position where you might deprive them of that privilege. And that is what you have done. Being drunk is one of the worst offences, if not the worst in the theatre, and I will not tolerate it in one of my shows. I loathe drunkenness. I have seen people drunk on stage and I simply won't tolerate it. Not even from a chorus girl.

BOY: I really am sorry, Mr Ivor. It was all my fault.

IVOR: Yes, I can see that. And you do seem suitably repentant. Have you been drinking too?

BOY: I'm far more used to it than...

IVOR: Don't finish that sentence, boy. No, otherwise I really will get mad.

BOY: I really am sorry, especially about Jen. And I think I've rather blown it with her now.

Beat.

IVOR: Really? You quite like this girl, then, I take it.

BOY: That wasn't why I took her...

IVOR: No indeed, no. But it is a shame, nevertheless, that you so nearly ruined everything for yourself, yes? Probably very politic you came to me.

BOY: I'm very sorry.

IVOR: Look, Duckie, I'll tell you what. Bring Jenny to my dressing room, and we'll let her sleep the rest of the evening off. Now, if you promise that this will never happen again, then I'll make sure no one gets to know about it. Is that enough of a gentleman's agreement for you?

BOY: I'll say.

IVOR walks closer to the young man.

IVOR: And perhaps, you and Jenny might like to travel down to Redroofs with me one weekend. Take in the country air, so to speak. A dip in the pool to take our minds off this dreadful war.

BOY: I'd like that very much.

Pause.

IVOR: Now you really ought to get changed.

BOY: Yes. And thank you. Thank you so much.

Pause.

IVOR: And don't forget about your girl. Now run along. (*Music starts to play. IVOR looks at the mirror.*)

IVOR: Silly boy.

Interlude C – Another scene from *The Dancing Years*

Lights come up on OLIVE and the LEADING LADY.

LADY & OLIVE (*sing* The Wings of Sleep):
        'Soon as the shades are falling
        Gently calling you to rest
        All the bright hours forgetting
        Slowly setting in the west...'

OLIVE (*sings*): 'Music begins to fill the sky
                With a slow lullaby...'

LADY & OLIVE (*sing*): 'Soothing and softly smoothing
                Cares away
                From the noisy day...'

IVOR exits his dressing room.

LADY (*sings*): 'When night is dark and deep
                And shepherds count their sheep...'

OLIVE (*sings*): 'You'll hear in the silver silence
                The whispering wings of sleep...'

LADY & OLIVE (*sing*): 'They fly around your bed
                And soothe your weary head
                So dream till dawn
                Securely borne
                On the wings of sleep...'

LADY (*sings*): 'When night is dark and deep
                And shepherds count their sheep...'

OLIVE (*sings*): 'You'll hear in the silver silence
                The whispering wings of sleep...'

LADY & OLIVE (*sing*): 'They fly around your bed
                And soothe your weary head
                So dream till dawn
                Securely borne
                On the wings of sleep
                The wings of sleep
                The wings of sleep.'

Scene Five

Ivor's dressing room, The Adelphi.

April 13th, 1944 – the evening after Ivor's trial. IVOR enters the dressing room. He sits at his table and looks at himself in the mirror. He then picks up a photograph of his mother.

IVOR: Mam, dear Mam. How I miss you. These past few months have been hell. Sheer, utter hell.

Beat.

IVOR: They're going to lock me up, Mam. They're going to lock me up. And for something so petty. So insignificant. I can hardly believe it. Mam? What am I going to do?

OLIVE enters the dressing room, followed by BOBBIE. There is silence as IVOR sits down on his bed.

OLIVE: Can I get you anything, Ivor? What about you?

BOBBIE: No thank you, I think we just need to get him ready for tonight's performance.

OLIVE: Are you staying?

BOBBIE: I think it would be best if I did. I haven't seen the show in a while, so it's about time I sat through the old dinosaur again. Besides, I could do with the sleep.

IVOR chuckles.

OLIVE: You are an awful individual.

BOBBIE: Someone has to be.

Silence.

OLIVE: I've some chocolates in my dressing room.

Silence.

OLIVE: Ivor?

BOBBIE: Well I want them, even if he doesn't.

OLIVE: I'll get... now, shall I? Ivor?

IVOR shrugs.

OLIVE: What exactly did he mean?

BOBBIE: What?

OLIVE: The Magistrate said, 'To a man like you' etc, etc – what's that supposed to mean? As if a fine wasn't enough. As if prison was the only alternative for a 'man like you'. What kind of a man is 'a man like you'?

BOBBIE: The kind who likes chocolates?

OLIVE: Yes, well, I thought the law treated everyone equally. That Magistrate treated Ivor worse than a common criminal.

BOBBIE: That magistrate was a prune.

OLIVE: Exactly.

BOBBIE: He had it in for Ivor before he even started. Although Ivor probably gave the worst performance of his life.

IVOR grunts.

BOBBIE: Not counting his films, of course.

OLIVE: Bobbie, really.

Beat.

OLIVE: I ought to get those chocolates.

LADY (*entering*): Oh, God, it's terrible. I heard it all from Popie, he seems quite distraught, it's going to be all over the newspapers. I didn't know what to say, I just came as soon as I could.

BOBBIE: You heard about the chocolates, then?

OLIVE: Bobbie! Ignore him, dear; he's being facetious, we're all glad to see you, especially Ivor.

LADY: How can he be found guilty? It's absurd. It's unthinkable that any one would think he had anything to do with that awful woman's... well, it doesn't bear thinking about.

IVOR: Maybe I should have just pleaded guilty.

BOBBIE: Poppycock. You weren't guilty and so you didn't plead guilty.

LADY: Quite right. If anyone should have pleaded guilty then it was that woman. She's the one who should have pleaded guilty.

OLIVE: She did plead guilty, dear.

Beat.

LADY: Really? Oh. Well, then, everyone pleaded whatever they should have pleaded and that should have been an end to it. It's all too horrible.

BOBBIE (*distracted*): Yes. Except she pleaded 'not guilty', Olive.

OLIVE: Did she?

BOBBIE: Yes, she merely decided not to speak in her defence. Funny how quickly we distort the details.

OLIVE: And for that she was fined fifty pounds while our Ivor is going to prison?

BOBBIE: He is not going to prison. Will everyone stop saying that he is going to prison. He merely had an awful day in court and some prune of a Magistrate has decided to set a very public and high profile example of Ivor Novello. So that others will take note. That's why we've been granted appeal, because everyone knows he is not going to prison, it's as simple as that.

LADY: How long till the appeal?

BOBBIE: A month, and by then we will have public support, the facts will be straightened out and this whole sorry mess will be sorted.

LADY: I couldn't bear it if you went to prison, Ivor, it would be too unspeakable.

IVOR kisses her gently.

LADY: I can't bear to think of you stood in that little dock. Didn't they take into account everything he's done?

OLIVE: I don't think this particular magistrate sees anything that Ivor has done as good or bad or even consequential.

IVOR: Olive, dear girl, we've been discussing the ins and outs of this sordid little day for nigh on five minutes. Five, minutes, no? And then suddenly, as if in a crescendo of understanding I realise something. A thing that I could not have hoped for in court, no, but that could now, very nearly save my life.

OLIVE: What is it, Ivor?

IVOR: The materialisation of this said little chocolate.

BOBBIE laughs.

OLIVE: Oh, you're worse than him.

LADY: Ivor, you're incorrigible, how can you joke when all this is going on?

IVOR: Because, my dear, I remembered how nothing could be ill in the world when there is beauty like yours. Now stop all this fuss, Bobbie's right, I'm not going to prison.

BOBBIE: Of course not. Eddie Marsh is personally going to complain to Churchill. He's livid. Everything will be fine.

IVOR: That is if, and only if, I get my chocolate, dear.

OLIVE: I'm just on my way. (*She leaves.*)

BOBBIE: I'll join you.

LADY (*to BOBBIE, as he is leaving*): This will all go away, won't it?

IVOR: Like a moth when you switch out the lights inside the house, and then turn on the lights to the porch. Isn't that right, darling? It will all go away, won't it, Bobbie?

BOBBIE: We'll talk about it at home.

IVOR: Can we not go home now, darling?

Silence. BOBBIE leaves.

LADY: Just awful rotten luck.

IVOR: Yes.

Beat.

IVOR: You know, she always seemed like a perfectly intelligent, harmless little woman. You wouldn't have thought she had it in her.

LADY: I can hardly remember her.

IVOR: Oh she was always there, M, you must remember her. She used to follow us around the country.

LADY: Really? But that's absurd.

IVOR: She told us it was her work. (*Sighs.*) But I suppose it gave her some little joy in an otherwise unexceptional life.

Beat.

IVOR: She always seemed a little sad to me.

LADY: Yes.

IVOR: I suppose I just felt a little sorry for her. And her devotion was absolute.

LADY: Yes.

IVOR: Sometimes she'd just appear, there, at the dressing room door and wait, hovering, until she'd had her few precious moments with me.

LADY: Just here.

IVOR: Yes. She always hovered there, just there. At the dressing room door.

LADY (*stood in the doorway*): Awful. Awful rotten luck. (*She exits.*)

Scene Six

Ivor's dressing room, The Adelphi.

April 1944, between the trial and the appeal. The Wings of Sleep *plays, as an instrumental piece. IVOR is sat at his dressing table. He looks into the mirror. BOBBIE enters.*

BOBBIE: You're here early. I woke up and you'd gone.

IVOR: I couldn't sleep this morning. So I came in early.

BOBBIE: Are you all right?

IVOR: Yes, I think so. I don't know. I was just thinking, that's all.

BOBBIE: And what were you thinking about?

IVOR: Love. Is that so shocking?

Beat.

IVOR: They are getting married. You know, the two lovebirds in the chorus. That adorably handsome couple: Eddie and that girl he's always with.

Beat.

BOBBIE: I've looked at today's papers. Your crime is pretty well covered by all of them.

IVOR: Of course no one is supposed to know it yet, but such is the speed of theatrical rumour, and so we must all act suitably surprised, but oh – to be that young and in love.

BOBBIE: Oh Ivor, shut up.

Beat.

IVOR: And what do the papers say this afternoon?

BOBBIE: What do you think they say?

IVOR: I don't think anymore.

BOBBIE: Well, I'm afraid it's bad news, Ivor.

FAN (*in the past*): I've got some wonderful news for you, Mr Ivor.

BOBBIE: They're painting you as rather a cad.

FAN (*in the past; brimming with excitement*): My firm... they've accepted the car.

BOBBIE: They seem to think that you tried to shift all the blame on to that woman.

IVOR (*to the FAN*): Really?

FAN (*in the past*): Yes, and I've got the nicest surprise for you. You know that we have a branch in Reading.

BOBBIE: Did you expect anything less from the papers?

IVOR (*to BOBBIE*): No, I didn't.

FAN (*in the past*): Well, we do, and so, any time you like, you can get a lift down to Littlewick.

IVOR (*to himself*): Even on a Saturday?

BOBBIE: What?

IVOR: I was just remembering something.

FAN (*in the past*): Yes, even on a Saturday. Why not? The car can always go to Reading on the Monday morning, if required. And it could call back on its way from Reading so that you can be back in town for Monday night.

IVOR: It was of course, too good to be true, her little plan.

BOBBIE: Of course.

FAN (*in the past*): That way, you can use the car as if it were your own again.

IVOR: Why did I insist on keeping Morgan on?

FAN (*in the past*): Well in that case, if you're willing to pay the chauffeur's salary yourself, I think they would be more than happy to let you keep him on.

IVOR: I just expected it to be above board. Just a simple arrangement. I wanted my car and then I had it.

FAN (*in the past*): You deserve the odd lift, Mr Ivor. After all, the car is part of the War effort now, isn't it?

IVOR: It seemed the most natural thing in the world.

FAN (*in the past*): And that's all down to you.

BOBBIE: Oh, how could you be so stupid? How could you put yourself in this position?

FAN (*in the past*): You deserve it, Mr Ivor.

IVOR: I don't know. If only I'd looked into it. Why didn't I take the time to look into it?

FAN (*in the past*): Oh yes, of course, I can see you're very busy. I'll come back after the show. I'm so glad you're pleased. It makes me very happy, you don't know how much. (*She exits.*)

IVOR: She was so happy to help me.

BOBBIE: And you let her do this to you. Why? How can you let these people into your life?

IVOR: Because without these people, none of us would have a career. Certainly not you.

Beat.

IVOR: I'm sorry, darling, I didn't mean that.

BOBBIE: I want you to really consider how serious this all is.

IVOR: I do, Bobbie, I do. But I have to get ready for the show now.

BOBBIE: It's not a question of being a little extravagant and wanting your car for the odd day. It's not even a question of a little petrol you were entitled to. They think of you as someone who conspired to break the law.

IVOR: But that's preposterous. I couldn't conspire to boil an egg. I'd be too afraid, for one thing.

BOBBIE: That's not how it looks, and I'm afraid in these things it's always a question of how it looks.

IVOR: Do you think?

BOBBIE: Yes, I think. This mess you've got your self into could have been avoided. You could have hired a private car. With a doctor's certificate you easily could have justified that. But no, you had to go and sort out this little scheme yourself. All for a stupid car journey or two.

IVOR: Don't be awful to me, please.

BOBBIE: Well I'm angry at you, all right! At your naivety.

IVOR: I always thought you were rather fond of my naivety... Mr Andrews.

BOBBIE: No, Mr Novello, I'm rather fond of you.

OLIVE (*entering, carrying a large bundle of letters*): I tried to get you at the flat but you had already left. There are hundreds of them. Hundreds of letters pouring in, every one of them declaring their absolute belief in your innocence. I shouldn't wonder that they'll be in their thousands by the time we've finished.

IVOR (*genuinely taken aback*): Really, all for me? How marvellous.

BOBBIE: Let's just hope the court feels the same way.

OLIVE: This is just the beginning, Gentleman, this is just the beginning.

The lights fade on them as IVOR enters the world of The Dancing Years.

Scene Seven

Ivor's dressing room, The Adelphi.

April 1944. Music starts to play. OLIVE and BOBBIE busy themselves, working through letters and documents.

OLIVE: Now that one is divine. Definitely today's winner. Come the interval that is the first one he sees. He simply must see that one.

BOBBIE: Olive, this woman is mad. Before we know it, she'll be giving birth to his child.

OLIVE: Oh you're hideous. They're his fans Bobbie. They're his whole world. He loves them. We have to respect that.

Interlude D – *The Dancing Years*

IVOR: Clever Maria!

LADY: Yes, Clever Maria!

IVOR: Well, I'm going to tell you something, clever Maria, because I'm drunk and my tongue is very loose – you know how grateful I am to you – hearing my music played and sung like that for the first time. But you must not take me for granted; exploit me at your will.

LADY: Surely you know I would never do that.

IVOR: Maria. Are you in love with me?

LADY: In love, Rudi?

IVOR: Yes. Something very exciting has happened and I don't know whether I can explain it. You and my music have become one, and as I love and respect my music, I must love and respect you.

LADY: But that's what I want. (*Sings* I Can Give You The Starlight:) 'When I was young my foolish fancies used to make
    A great mistake
    But now a little love, a little living
    Has changed my ways and taught me
    And brought me
    The joy of giving
    I can give you the starlight
    Love unchanging and true
    I can give you the ocean
    Deep and tender devotion
    I can give you the mountains
    Pools of shimmering blue
    Call and I shall be
    All you ask of me
    Music in spring, flowers for a king
    All these I bring to you.'

BOBBIE: Were there any other letters today?

OLIVE: Only a few. Not enough to register.

BOBBIE: And how were they?

OLIVE: Hateful.

Scene Eight

Ivor's dressing room, The Adelphi.

May 1944. There is a knock at the door.

IVOR: Come in. (*The BOY comes in.*) Oh it's you. Come in, please. How are you dear boy?

BOY: Actually, I've never been better.

IVOR: Really? I'm glad to hear it.

Beat.

IVOR: But...

Pause.

IVOR: Look, what is it I can do for you?

BOY: Well, I hope it's not too much to ask, what with all the trouble that you're having right now, but...

IVOR: Am in any trouble? Me, Ivor Novello, wanton criminal, last seen with Bonnie & Clyde. How I adore dear Bonnie, lovely singing voice.

BOY: Maybe I should come at another time.

IVOR: Don't be foolish, I'm only teasing you. I haven't lost my mind quite yet. Now, where's that lovely girl of yours?

BOY: Actually she was too shy to come.

IVOR: Why, what has she done this time? Has she jumped ship for some lewd French review?

BOY: Nothing like that, she just thought it better if I came myself. We're going to get married.

IVOR: My dear boy, that's marvellous. I had no idea.

BOY: No, we've tried to keep it a secret, just tell a few close friends. But we were wondering if...

IVOR: I hope you haven't planned this for when I'm prison. I do so adore weddings.

BOY: Oh, you won't go to prison, Ivor.

Beat.

IVOR: If you say so.

Pause.

IVOR: Please, have a seat.

BOY: Thank you.

Beat.

BOY: We were wondering... well... we would very much like one of your songs sung at the reception.

IVOR: How wonderful. Which song?

BOY: *My Life Belongs To You.*

IVOR: And what a marvellous choice. It's yours.

BOY: Thank you, thank you so much again.

IVOR: It's really nothing, it's not as if I'm paying for the wedding, it's just a song. But if you have any trouble in that, do let me know, won't you?

BOY: Yes, thank you, but Jen's parents are quite well to do, I think.

IVOR: Good for her. Good for her. My parents were rather, well...

Beat.

IVOR: No. No, I want you to tell me, why that song, especially?

BOY: Because I fell in love with it the first time I heard it. Because ever since I heard it, it's been my favourite in the whole show. And Jenny feels the same. We sing it to each other sometimes.

IVOR: How marvellous. But I don't remember you auditioning? To understudy, I mean?

BOY: I don't feel I'm really up to the job, sir. I mean, for our wedding perhaps, but...

IVOR: Nonsense, I'm sure you're up to it. So now then, here's your chance, cheer my spirits a little. Sing some of it for me.

BOY: Now?

IVOR: Yes, now, indulge me a little. Think of it as an audition. For your wedding day. (*He lies back and closes his eyes.*)

Silence.

IVOR: You can start whenever you want.

BOY (*smiles, sings*): 'When first we met
                    I heard a voice within
                    "The scene is set
                    And here's your heroine"
                    I raised my eyes,
                    My breath was taken
                    By that sweet surprise.'

Pause.

IVOR (*spoken*): 'Your hand was mine
                  By law divine.'
    Did you know I was nearly married once?

BOY: Yes of course, to Gladys Cooper. Everyone knows it.

IVOR: Never would have worked.

BOY: No.

IVOR: Our temperaments are too different, don't you think?

BOY: Yes. I know.

IVOR: And how do you know, dear boy?

BOY: Well, because I saw you.

IVOR (*sitting up*): When did you see me?

BOY: When I was a boy, Mr Ivor. When you were filming Bonnie Prince Charlie.

IVOR: Good heavens, you couldn't have been more than two at the time.

BOY: I was nine. We both share that gift of looking younger than we are.

IVOR: You've a great career ahead of you, haven't you?

Beat.

IVOR: Tell me about Bonnie Prince Charlie.

BOY: We went to stay with an aunt, when you were on location. We were only a few miles away and we used to go up to watch sometimes. You always came and chatted to the fans between takes, whereas Miss Cooper kept herself to herself. My mum was never that keen on her after that. Always seemed a bit aloof to my mum.

IVOR: Not aloof, no. She just liked her privacy, that's all.

BOY: But you always had time for us. Mum said that's why you never married Gladys Cooper, because of us. Because you were too in love with your fans.

48

IVOR: That's why, then. Now I understand.

BOY: My mother was a great follower of yours after that. She even had your signature framed and placed in the hall.

IVOR (*laughs*): The hall? I gave up wedded bliss for you and I didn't even make it to the mantelpiece?

BOY: I suppose that was wrong of her, but, well...

IVOR: Of course we both know my fans are not the reason I couldn't marry, don't we, dear boy?

BOY: Of course. But I think my mother's theory makes sense to her.

IVOR: And so it should.

Beat.

BOY: She wanted me to grow up to be just like you.

IVOR: Indeed.

BOY: And I knew that I wanted to do this. I knew that I wanted to be just like you. And privacy... well, some things you have to sacrifice for the job.

IVOR: No matter what happens?

BOY: Yes. I believe that. I have to.

IVOR (*lying back again*): You didn't finish your song.

Pause.

BOY (*sings*): 'Your hand was mine
                By law divine
                My life belongs to you
                My dreams, my songs, all that I do
                No moon, no morning star can shine
                No happiness is mine
                Without you.'

BOBBIE enters. The BOY stops singing.

IVOR: Is that Mr Andrews?

BOY: Yes.

IVOR: You'd better leave, then.

BOY: Yes, of course, and thank you again. Jen will be thrilled. (*He exits.*)

BOBBIE: I told you that boy was very 'musical'.

IVOR: That boy is head over heels in love.

BOBBIE: So it would appear.

IVOR: Don't be a bore, Bobbie. He's getting married.

BOBBIE: How wonderful.

IVOR: It is wonderful, yes!

Beat.

BOBBIE: Well I have some other wonderful news. I've just come from the solicitors. Fred Allen is going to give character testimony at the hearing.

IVOR: But he's ill. He's under doctor's orders.

BOBBIE: You know Freddie. He'd come on a stretcher if you'd have him.

IVOR: But that's marvellous. Where's Olive?

BOBBIE: She's on her way up. You know, public support is finally swinging our way.

IVOR: Really?

BOBBIE: Yes.

IVOR: So now we wait.

BOBBIE: Now we wait.

Beat.

IVOR: And that's the hardest part. I've never had to wait for anything in my whole life. It's been like a constant whirlwind. And all I have ever done was to try and make people happy, to just take them away from whatever life they have, just for a little while.

BOBBIE: I know that.

IVOR: So why is this happening to me? I feel like all this, all this work is going to end, because of a little petrol.

51

BOBBIE: It's not going to end.

IVOR: Yes it is. If I go to prison, that is the end. I'm finished. I won't recover from the shame. How could I? They'll never let me forget it.

BOBBIE: Which is precisely why you have to carry on. You are an innocent man, and so you must carry on as if nothing has changed, as if this whole sordid little thing has never happened.

IVOR: I was hoping you'd reassure me that I wouldn't go to prison. Mr Andrews.

BOBBIE: Well, I can assure you that you shouldn't. The important thing is to make sure that you keep your spirits up. Laugh a little.

IVOR: I have been laughing.

BOBBIE: No you haven't. Not inside. Not with your eyes.

IVOR: And suddenly you're a poet?

BOBBIE: If you say so.

OLIVE (*entering*): Have you told him? About Freddie?

BOBBIE: Indeed I have.

OLIVE: He makes our full set of aces, Ivor. Four ace witnesses. Freddie, Sir Edward, Dame Sybil Thorndike and her delightfully droll husband Sir Lewis Casson are all going to give testimony on your behalf.

IVOR: Why, that's wonderful news.

OLIVE: I know. Sir Lewis said that on this rare occasion he was more than willing to publicly agree with his wife.

IVOR laughs.

OLIVE: I think we can win this time, gentleman.

IVOR: You really think so?

OLIVE: Yes, because this time all the facts will come out. For instance, you reported the irregularities to the Petrol Board the moment you knew anything was wrong.

BOBBIE: Hardly the act of a guilty man.

OLIVE: Exactly. And besides, if that woman had acquired the licence legally, if she really had been as important at her firm as she said she was

BOBBIE: Instead of lying incessantly.

OLIVE: Then your lifts would have been perfectly acceptable to the Petrol Board.

IVOR: So?

BOBBIE: So if her boss had been aware of the car.

OLIVE: If the facts had been as you believed them to be at the time.

BOBBIE: Then no breach of the law would have taken place.

OLIVE: Which means you didn't knowingly do anything wrong.

BOBBIE: Even Churchill has said he thinks it's an appalling travesty. It's just a shame he can't intervene.

OLIVE: Yes.

BOBBIE: And then, of course, there are the earrings.

OLIVE: Yes. That woman does have Mam's earrings.

IVOR: But she asked for them.

OLIVE: We know that, but she says they were a present for getting you the car. (*To BOBBIE:*) It's her word against his.

BOBBIE: So it all comes down to your performance in the witness box.

OLIVE: Yes, but this time he'll be prepared.

IVOR: I am not giving a performance, darlings, I'm simply telling the truth.

BOBBIE: We are not talking about truth; we're talking about the law. And you are possibly one of the worst witnesses any of us have ever seen.

OLIVE: I can't really say I've spent much time in a courtroom, Bobbie. But he is right, darling, you did seem terribly ill at ease.

BOBBIE: So this time you'll have to be calm when you're cross-examined. That's vital.

IVOR: Yes.

OLIVE: Vital.

IVOR: Yes, yes. God, I think I'm going to be sick. (*He rushes out.*)

OLIVE: Too much excitement?

BOBBIE: Too much excitement.

OLIVE: I'll see to it.

BOBBIE: Thank you. (*She rushes out, after IVOR.*)

Scene Nine

Ivor's dressing room, The Adelphi.

May 15th, 1944. The evening before the Appeal.

BOBBIE is alone. The strain of the past month has affected him also and he puts his head in his hands.

Interlude E – *The Dancing Years*

The LEADING LADY leans on the piano as IVOR plays.

LADY: And now let's do some work. I can't get the last page of that gavotte, have you got it there?

IVOR: No, but I've got something else I'd like you to try.

LADY: Oh?

IVOR: Something I wrote last night.

LADY: Oh, I know, another waltz.

IVOR: No, no, not another waltz, no. This is just a simple little tune. Not a money maker. I wrote the words, too. See if you like it.

LADY: It's dedicated to me.

BOBBIE looks up.

IVOR: They're all dedicated to you.

LADY (*trying to read Ivor's writing*): Oh, Rudi, you're writing. Really, say them for me, I don't want to spoil it.

*As IVOR speaks, BOBBIE starts to cry, and the LEADING LADY hums the music until point * – when she stops.*

IVOR: My dearest dear
        If I could say to you
        In words as clear
        As when I play to you,
        You'd understand
        How slight the shadow that is holding us apart...*
(*He looks at the LEADING LADY.*)
        So take my hand
        I'll lead the way for you
        A little waiting and you'll reach my heart.

The light fades on The Dancing Years. *The dressing room is still lit.*

BOBBIE stands. IVOR and OLIVE enter.

BOBBIE: How was it?

IVOR: I think that may have been my last ever performance of Rudi Kleber in *The Dancing Years*.

BOBBIE: Poppycock, and you know it.

OLIVE: Ivor was wonderful. And he'll be playing again tomorrow night, too.

IVOR: No, not tomorrow night, no. Whatever happens, I think I deserve tomorrow night off, don't you?

OLIVE: Celebrating till four in the morning?

IVOR: Five at least.

BOBBIE: Do I hear any advance on six?

They laugh. Then silence.

IVOR: I tried to bribe that police officer, why did I do that?

OLIVE: It was hardly what you'd call a bribe.

IVOR: But it was, really. What an extraordinary thing to do. He stood there and I asked if this whole thing could be kept quiet. I just didn't want it in the papers. And he just shook his head and left. Why did I do that?

OLIVE: The only thing that you've been guilty of is poor judgement, Ivor. And we all are guilty of that.

BOBBIE: I'm not.

They look at him.

BOBBIE: Ivor. Darling. You won't go to prison.

IVOR: I think if you say it enough times, it eventually becomes true.

BOY (*popping his head into dressing room*): Can I come in?

OLIVE: Yes, of course.

BOY (*entering, with a towel around his neck and carrying a card*): I'm sorry, I just wanted to bring you this. It's just a little card from the cast. To wish you good luck. (*To BOBBIE:*) It wasn't my idea; one of the other boys thought it would be nice.

IVOR: Thank you, it's very sweet... of you.

BOY: Good luck for tomorrow, Mr Ivor.

OLIVE: Thank you.

BOY: And well done for tonight. We all thought you were smashing.

IVOR: Thank you. (*The BOY leaves. IVOR is opening the card:*) Look, it's beautiful, isn't it? I don't know what to say. I simply adore it. This is a good sign, isn't it? The best sign I've had all day.

OLIVE: It's a good sign. Now, we'll wait for you outside, darling, don't be too long. Come along Bobbie.

IVOR: Thank you. Both of you, for being here.

BOBBIE: Oh we'll always be here.

OLIVE: Yes, always. Bobbie, myself.

BOBBIE: Your leading ladies.

OLIVE: Bobbie, we're each his leading lady, aren't we darling?

IVOR: Yes. Always.

OLIVE: Now come along. (*BOBBIE and OLIVE exit. IVOR stands in the middle of his dressing room and looks around. He raises his arms as if to welcome it in to him. Then he drops them again.*)

Interlude F – *The Dancing Years*

IVOR (*speaks*): 'So take my hand
              I'll lead the way for you
              A little waiting and you'll reach my heart.'

LADY (*sighs*): Play it through. (*She sings* My Dearest Dear:)
              'My dearest dear
              If I could say to you
              In words as clear
              As when I play to you
              You'd understand
              How slight the shadow that is keeping us apart
              So take my hand
              I'll lead the way for you
              A little waiting and you'll reach my heart....'

Instrumental section.

BOBBIE enters the dressing room.

BOBBIE: Ivor? Are you all right?

IVOR: I don't know. I really don't know.

BOBBIE: Come on. Let's go home.

BOBBIE exits. IVOR goes to follow, but stops at the door to the dressing room, and looks back in.

LADY (*sings*): 'You'd understand
How slight the shadow that is keeping us apart
So take my hand
I'll lead the way for you
A little waiting and you'll reach my heart.'

The light fades as the LEADING LADY and IVOR exit.

ACT TWO
Scene One

Prison Cell No. 242, Wormwood Scrubs.

A prison cell. There are two small tables – one bearing washing utensils; a mattress to sleep on; a large heavy earthenware pint mug, an enamel bowl and a plate; a tin knife, a fork and a spoon, and a tin can. Music is playing. IVOR appears at the door to the cell. He enters. OLIVE and the FAN appear in a spotlight. They speak the following lines over each other; oblivious to each other.

OLIVE: Ivor dearest...

FAN: He's trying to put all the blame on me...

OLIVE: I'll do everything I can to make sure people know what a...

FAN: That's grossly unfair...

OLIVE: Travesty of justice this is. I promise that with all my heart.

FAN: When he received the permit...

OLIVE: By the time you get out...

FAN: He was really thrilled...

OLIVE: Not a single person will think you are guilty of anything at all...

FAN: And said I could have anything in the world I wanted...

OLIVE: I promise it. Not a soul.

FAN: Anything.

The light fades on them. BOBBIE appears.

BOBBIE: Ivor. It's me speaking – Mr Andrews. I want you to listen, and listen carefully to me. This is absolutely nothing. Do you hear me, nothing. It's only one month. At least we halved it to that. So the appeal wasn't a complete failure.

Beat.

BOBBIE: One month. It will pass.

Lights up on IVOR, in his cell.

IVOR (*eyes lowered*): Ivor Novello.

Pause.

IVOR: Actor – Manager.

A spotlight on the PADRE.

PADRE: Isn't that lucky, now, Governor, this is the very chap for us. He can give us some advice and help about that stage...

IVOR looks up.

PADRE: We are building. Yes, that's right, Mr Novello, we are building a stage. Would you like to help us?

The light fades on the PADRE and he enters Ivor's cell.

PADRE: Good morning, Ivor.

IVOR (*in himself*): Padre.

PADRE: You haven't eaten anything.

IVOR: No.

PADRE: You will need to eat, Mr Novello.

IVOR: Ivor.

PADRE: Ivor. Of course. Well, I'm sorry it's not what you're used to, but you will have to eat. If you are going to be of any use to us in the library...

IVOR looks up.

PADRE (*continuing*): You will need to eat. Yes, that's right, I've had a word with the Governor and he agreed that you'd probably be most help to us in the library. I know you'll be helping us with the stage, too, but in the meantime I thought we could put you to work in the library.

IVOR: Thank you.

PADRE: I don't see you being of much use to us anywhere else. And I'm aware that you are not the sort of man we're used to in here.

IVOR looks up at him.

PADRE: But you really must try and eat something.

Pause.

PADRE: Ivor, I think we both know that you shouldn't be here. And I'm quite sure Judge McKenna has done you a great injustice. I also understand that you are not well. But you must eat something.

IVOR: This blanket is dirty.

PADRE: Not something his Majesty should be proud of, but I'm afraid that's how it is, here.

Pause.

IVOR: I must get used to it.

PADRE: Yes.

IVOR: Things are worse in Europe.

Beat.

IVOR: Some of my company have left me for the War effort.

PADRE: From *The Dancing Years*?

IVOR: If you like. We've been at it so long, now, we think of it as *The Advancing Years*.

PADRE: You must have opened just before this dreadful war started.

IVOR: With dear Mary Ellis.

PADRE: Yes, I know.

IVOR: Did you see her?

PADRE: I'm afraid not.

IVOR: Wonderful.

Beat.

IVOR: She was mine for Glamorous Nights, too. What a dear, dear friend. I met her just after the Great War.

PADRE: I see.

IVOR: When I was no one, really.

PADRE: A no one from Cardiff, I believe?

IVOR: Yes, but I left when I was only a boy.

PADRE: You've still got a lilt, though.

IVOR: Beg your pardon?

PADRE: Well, there's no mistaking your background.

IVOR: Nor yours, Padre.

PADRE: So, where does the Novello come from?

IVOR: My grandfather. He once heard Clara Novello sing, and so named my mother after her.

PADRE: I see.

IVOR: She sang, too. With her choir.

PADRE: Yes.

IVOR: She was marvellous; she was so grand. Crowds would meet her at Cardiff Station, you know. Crowds.

PADRE: And your father?

IVOR (*stares at the PADRE*): Oh, you'd have liked my father.

PADRE: Really?

IVOR: Oh yes, he was such a gentle man – in the truest sense of the word. He was solid. Welsh.

The PADRE smiles.

IVOR: The very opposite to my mother. She was headstrong and wild, a real character, but he was quiet, an observer of our lives. Solid, content to be there in the background.

PADRE: And do you feel a great affinity with Wales?

IVOR: Strange, I feel most Welsh when people assume I'm not.

PADRE: In here, no one assumes anything, Ivor. But I think the other prisoners all know who you are, by now.

IVOR: I don't wish to be treated differently on account of who I am.

PADRE: I can't really predict how the men of Wormwood will treat Ivor Novello, but I'm sure you'll have no trouble while you're here.

IVOR: But what am I to do here? I mean in the library. I'm not an intellectual, you see. I simply know theatre, that's all.

PADRE: Well, that's the beauty of the job that I have in mind for you, Mr Novello. A number of the inmates here are not even literate, let alone intellectual. However, they all like looking at pictures. In fact most of the ones who can read prefer to look at the pictures, especially those pictures that are of sport, or indeed the celebrities that drift within your circles. So, in our own sweet way we are a prison full of stargazers.

IVOR: I don't understand, what I am to do?

PADRE: I would like you to make scrapbooks for them. I will make sure that you get to see all the illustrated papers, so that you can decide what your fellow inmates might want to see. Picture Post and the like. Then you can cut out pictures and paste them into scrapbooks. You will like doing that, I'm certain, and they will like looking at them.

IVOR: I see.

PADRE: Yes, you might even develop a little Wormwood fan club.

IVOR: Yes.

The FAN appears in a spotlight.

FAN: I, Dora Grace Constable. Known to you as Grace Walton, wish to confess that I have consistently lied to you about my position with Mr C W Heywood.

IVOR: Do you think it's easy to forgive, Padre?

PADRE: Do you want people to forgive you for something you haven't done?

IVOR: I don't know what I think, anymore. I'm sleeping on a dirty blanket. I'm not used to that.

FAN: Furthermore I have stolen approximately £1,100 from him and used his money to further my involvement with you.

PADRE: No. I think people will be appalled by this, if not now then soon. And I think it's a lot harder to forget than to forgive. Well, I suppose I'd better get you some pictures.

IVOR: Thank you for that.

PADRE: But please eat something.

FAN: I undertake never to approach you in any way whatsoever again, as long as I live.

The light fades on the FAN.

PADRE: And try not to think too much about the conditions here. The time will pass quickly.

The PADRE leaves the cell.

Scene Two

Prison Cell No. 242, Wormwood Scrubs.

A Medley of music from The Dancing Years *is heard as IVOR paces up and down the cell.*

IVOR(*as Rudi*): Maria, there's not much time and I have so many things to say. I love you and only you. You have always been the colour and the magic in my life and nothing can ever...

IVOR stops. His MAM appears behind him.

MAM: Ivor, how do you like this dress? I want your opinion. Do you think it fits behind?

IVOR (*reaching out to her, but she is gone*): Mam! (*He stares after her, then sits on his bed. He starts to sew a mailbag as he continues.*) There is so much unrest and unhappiness in the world. We are going to see great changes. We will almost forget to smile and make music, but not quite. I know, I feel it. One day, we'll wake as if from an evil dream and forget to hate, and the world will smile again and music and friendship will once more be important.

The sound of a cell door slamming shut. IVOR throws the mailbag on the floor.

Scene Three

Prison Cell No. 242, Wormwood Scrubs.

PADRE: Ivor. Ivor, Are you all right?

IVOR (*a little stunned*): What? I...

Beat.

IVOR: I can't do this.

PADRE (*picking up the bag*): Yes, you're quite right, you can't. This is bloody awful.

IVOR (*looking at the PADRE*): I can't sew. (*He raises his trembling hands.*) Why can't they sew?

PADRE: My wife could tell you. She's a hopeless sewer, herself.

Pause. IVOR looks up at the PADRE, confused. He coughs.

PADRE: Of course, you'll have to do some sort of homework. We need something to occupy your time here. But maybe we can arrange for you to be doing your scrapbooks. They're rather good, too.

IVOR: More scrapbooks? (*Coughs.*)

PADRE: That cough's a worry.

IVOR: It's just a cough.

PADRE: And you are also losing weight, which concerns me. You really do need to eat more. Would you not feel better in the infirmary?

IVOR: No. I don't need to be in an infirmary. What I need is a hot bath.

PADRE: Yes.

IVOR: Once a week, we have a bath, and they've drawn a red line around the inside of the bath and that is how much hot water we are allowed. It's quite the filthiest thing. (*Coughs.*) And yet I know it's only for a month. Some of the poor souls here talk so bravely about the next five or six years.

PADRE: And how are you getting on with the other men?

Beat.

IVOR: I think, all right. I am certainly meeting a colourful bunch of friends. One of the men told me he'd been accused of biting a prison guard's ear off.

PADRE: And do you think he did it?

IVOR: Oh, I know he did it. He flushed it down the toilet. Said ear is now somewhere between here and the Isle of Wight. (*Coughs.*) You know, I always thought of myself as someone who was not too fussy about a great many things, but I am. I like sleeping in a clean bed. I may be less of a man for that, but it is the only man I know how to be. And I have this terrible nagging doubt in my head that this would all be bearable if it weren't for the cold. Isn't that silly? You see, I've not been warm once, since I came here.

PADRE: No?

IVOR: No. The bed is a target for all the draughts.

PADRE: But what is so wrong in that, in being concerned about the cold?

IVOR: Well, I would hate for my main complaint to be a matter of the weather. (*Coughs.*) That would be so dreadfully commonplace. That really this crisis, this test of my sanity, is whether I should like a hot bath or not. What kind of a man does that make me?

PADRE: More than likely, a human one.

IVOR: Do you think? I'm not so sure. You see, I still think this illusion will come to an end. Like a child. It's a child's right, is it not? It's his birthright. (*Coughs.*) I'm sorry. I am a romantic, Padre. I've never been interested in people thinking me wonderfully deep or clever. I just... well, I write what I write. But then you've not really seen much of what I've written.

PADRE: No.

IVOR (*coughs*): Good for you.

PADRE: Of course, my wife is a huge admirer of yours.

IVOR: Even now?

PADRE: Especially now. Your friends are making great strides on your behalf. I think most people can see what a terrible injustice this is.

Pause.

IVOR: Do you believe in ghosts, Padre?

PADRE: Ghosts?

IVOR: Yes. I thought I saw my mother, stood there. She only said a word or two to me and then she was gone. But I suppose you must think it was my imagination: as a man of God. Or am I just going insane?

PADRE: There's a lot I shouldn't really comment on. After all, I truly believe the world was created in seven days. Many would call me insane for that.

IVOR: In here they would. Yes. (*Coughs.*) Excuse me.

PADRE: Ivor, listen to me. You may not be a man of God, but you are a man of music and I was wondering if you could help us at choir practice.

IVOR: Choir practice?

PADRE: Of course you know we have a choir here, too. You might even conduct for us, if you'd like that is.

IVOR (*coughs*): Conduct the choir?

PADRE: Well it's not Covent Garden, exactly, but we have the makings of a respectable sing along at a public house.

Beat.

PADRE: Now, what do you say?

IVOR: I'd like to help in anyway I can.

PADRE: I'll make a deal with you, then. No more mail bags. I think, for the safety of the British mail system, you really ought not to be sewing anything.

IVOR laughs, and coughs.

PADRE: Instead, you can continue your scrapbooks – but you help with the choir and the music for Sunday service.

IVOR (*looks out his window*): And could I teach them some new music?

PADRE: If you like. You might even like to play something for us.

IVOR: I would like that, yes. (*Coughs, still staring out of the window.*) That would be marvellous.

The PADRE exits.

IVOR: But I think with all its beauty I shall always hate the month of May.

The lights dim and Ivor's music plays. The sound of a cell slamming shut is heard. BOBBIE appears in a spotlight.

BOBBIE: I can't explain it to you. Not in any way that makes sense. It's just one of those misfortunes that happens to us all. Keep your head up there in the clouds and get through this. It will pass and you will be the better and the stronger for it because everyone believes in you! I want you to remember that. Every single minute you are in this unfortunate position, I want you to remember we will be working for you. And I promise you this: your welcome home will be greater than you ever imagined. It's only one month. It will pass.

Scene Four

Prison Cell No. 242, Wormwood Scrubs.

IVOR is pacing up and down his cell, playing Rudi.

Interlude G – *The Dancing Years*

A spot comes up on the LEADING LADY, who is onstage at the Adelphi, playing Maria.

IVOR: Clever Maria!

LADY: Yes, clever Maria!

IVOR: Well, I'm going to tell you something, clever Maria, because I'm drunk and my tongue is very loose – you know how grateful I am to you – hearing my music played and sung like that for the first time. But you must not take me for granted, exploit me at your will.

LADY: Surely you know I would never do that.

IVOR: Maria. Are you in love with me?

LADY: In love, Rudi?

IVOR: Yes. Something very exciting has happened and I don't know whether I can explain it. You and my music have become one, and as I love and respect my music. I must love and respect you.

LADY: But that's what I want.(*Sings:*)
        'When I was young my foolish fancies used to make...'

The sound of a cell door slamming shut. IVOR jolts and the LEADING LADY disappears. IVOR sits for a moment and then stands again.

IVOR: Well, I'm going to tell you something, clever Maria, because I'm drunk and my tongue is very loose – you know how grateful I am to you.

Another cell door slams shut. This time, IVOR puts his hands over his ears.

IVOR: Yes. Something very exciting has happened and I don't know whether I can explain it. You and my music have become one, and...

Another cell door slams shut.

IVOR: Oh, God! God! (*He lies down on his mattress and starts to work on a scrap book.*)

Scene Five

Prison Cell No. 242, Wormwood Scrubs.

MAM: Ivor, how do you like this dress? I want your opinion. Do you think it fits, behind?

IVOR(*confused*): Mam.

MAM: Were you sleeping, dear? It's time to get up. We've so much to do. Don't you know there could be a war any moment?

IVOR: Mam?

MAM: Now where do you keep the hot water? I'm quite parched. We'll need some lemon too, darling, for the tea. Or a little sugar?

IVOR: There is no sugar, Mam.

MAM: Not even a little sugar for your dearest Mam? Ivor, it's really unforgivable. Now, I have so many lessons to give this morning, I really can't stay long. But I want you to be the first to know. I've wonderful news. We're going to march on Berlin.

IVOR: Berlin, Mam?

MAM: Yes, we shall make Hitler see some sense. A little melody and the rich soil of Glamorgan should do the trick.

IVOR: But we're already at war, Mam.

MAM: No dear, not at all. This will be my greatest conquest. I've always loved conquest, dear.

IVOR: Yes.

MAM: And this will be my greatest. My greatest obstacle overcome. We'll be like Napoleon marching over the Alps. And the sun will be in their eyes, Ivor, so they won't see us coming.

IVOR: No, Mam.

MAM: Sixty, that's how many I'll take. I'll take sixty of my girls, and we'll move right on down to Berlin. The Hague – that's where we'll start – and then Holland, Belgium and finally, Berlin.

IVOR: Singing for Peace.

MAM: Yes, darling, what a wonderful idea. 'Singing for Peace.' That will be our slogan. You're so wonderful with your titles, dear. And then we'll show them what a band of welsh Women can really do. We'll wear costumes, traditional welsh costumes, made from the finest linen and silk. And then, when we reach Berlin, we'll wear white lace – white angels singing for peace. And we'll release hundreds and hundreds of doves – no, better still, pigeons. Pigeons with messages tied to their feet; each with a message of peace to carry all over the world. And then Hitler will see how silly he's being and he'll call off his troops, and the world will see the wonderful things it's starting to forget.

IVOR (*upset*): Mam. How I miss you, Mam.

MAM: Darling boy, why are you crying? It's only a short time till we'll be together again. Only a little while. Now, you must take your singing lessons seriously, and listen to your masters.

IVOR: Masters.

MAM (*oblivious*): Oxford. My darling boy, at Oxford. I knew you'd win that singing scholarship. I don't know what your father was thinking, but I knew it.

IVOR: Yes, Mam.

MAM: And you'll be singing solo before you know it. By the time you're twelve, we'll see.

IVOR: Yes.

MAM: Now, no more tears, darling. I'll send you a big hamper at the weekend. With shortbread and potted meats, and jam. Perhaps a little chocolate or two? You deserve them, darling. You only deserve the best, my darling, beautiful son.

IVOR: All taken so much for granted. Even a single chocolate.

MAM: No sugar? Not even a little drop of lemon for the mother of Ivor Novello.

IVOR: I think you must go now, Mam.

MAM: Not until you give me the four thousand pounds I need.

IVOR: For what?

MAM: Have you listened to a word I've said? For our march on Hitler. At least.

IVOR: Mam, I must finish this.

MAM (*snatching the scrapbook from him*): No.

IVOR: Give it to me.

MAM: No, I will not. You've an opera to compose. You'll be conducting an opera soon, I'm sure of it. And I'm preparing for battle. We can't... we haven't the time to worry about the silliness of... (*dropping the scrap book*). Why is this room so drab? Ivor, have you lost your mind?

IVOR: Please go.

MAM: Not until you kiss my hand and swear devotion to me.

IVOR: I can't, Mam, I can't.

MAM: Nonsense. Of course you can. If you put your mind to it you can do anything. My ladies have sung for her Majesty the Queen, God rest her soul. These arms can testify to that. These arms that have been kissed by Saint-Saens. This wonderful left arm. 'It has magic in it.' That's what he said, darling, Saint-Saens. Magic. And some of that magic has found its way into you, my darling child. My dearest boy.

IVOR: I'm finished, Mam.

Ivor's MAM goes to touch his hair, but falters.

MAM (*exiting, sings Keep The Home Fires Burning*):
    'There's a silver lining
    Through the dark clouds shining...'
    (*she hums the next two lines*).

IVOR (*voice trembling, sings*): 'Turn the dark clouds inside out
                    Till the boys...'
                    (*he picks up the scrapbook*).

Scene Six

Prison Cell No. 242, Wormwood Scrubs.

Ivor's music plays in the background. IVOR is pacing up and down his cell.

IVOR: Clever Maria! Clever Maria!

The LEADING LADY does not appear, so IVOR starts to play both Rudi and Maria, in The Dancing Years.

IVOR: Yes, clever Maria!

IVOR: Well, I'm going to tell you something, clever Maria, because I'm drunk and my tongue is very loose – you know how grateful I am to you – hearing my music played and sung... like that for the first time. But you must not take me for granted, exploit me at your will.

IVOR: Surely you know I would never do that?

IVOR: No! No! No!

IVOR falls to the floor, distraught. A spotlight appears on BOBBIE.

BOBBIE: And I promise you this: your welcome home will be greater than you ever imagined. It's only one month. It will pass. It will.

Beat.

BOBBIE: But I do miss you. I stayed in again, last night. Couldn't sleep. I'm so used to going out at night it's strange to be home so early. But I find it impossible to enjoy myself when I know you're in that God forsaken place. But you'll be home soon. And I will be there for you. Always.

IVOR is rocking back and forth, holding his hands over his ears, sobbing. The PADRE enters, near him.

PADRE: Ivor? Ivor?

IVOR moans.

PADRE: Ivor, listen to me. The Deputy Governor has sent me to see you. Do you need the doctor? Do you want me to call the doctor?

IVOR: No. (*Looks up.*) I'm finished!

PADRE: Ivor. You are not finished. You have only a fortnight to go until this is all over.

IVOR: And then what? What am I to do then? My career, all my ambitions are over. My whole reason. I cannot... face the world. Oh, it's fine in here, locked away from reality – I must retire from the theatre – worrying how to fill each day. But when this is over there is nothing! I must leave the stage forever. How can I live? This shame. I'd give it all to the war effort if I could – I have money, plenty of it, thousands of pounds, but how can I live? If I could turn back the clock and not live through...

PADRE: There is no shame, Ivor.

IVOR: Then what is there? I've done nothing but think, since.... And if I do come out of this sane – Christ Jesus, help me to get through this and come out sane! They locked that door this afternoon. What is there for me?

PADRE: Ivor, it's all right.

IVOR: No, it's not. (*Coughs.*) Oh, heavens, I think the root of all insanity is boredom. I feel almost – except that – nothing, anymore. Sheer, utter futile black boredom. And once the stunned feeling... I see what's ahead of me, and I see nothing. Oh I might as well be dead. The nothingness, fades and then...

82

PADRE: Ivor, you still have so much more to give.

IVOR: What have I ever given anyone? Romance has poured out of me – really – since I was... but even that is a fraud, an illusion. I haven't a truly – since I was a child – romance! I can't even... no. There's this boy, Eddie. I mean, this couple. Such a lovely young man. They're getting married and I... what is it I want? They are so blissfully in love and I think I want whatever... this dream they live, I... why can't I just be happy for them? But of course what I really want is... I am, of course, very happy. I do know what it's like to be in love. You see, when I met my friend, Bobbie, I...

Pause.

PADRE: Ivor, there are some things I don't understand. Some things I choose not to understand. But that has no bearing on you being here.

IVOR: Doesn't it?

PADRE: You have done nothing wrong.

IVOR: How can you be so sure? I think of all those young men – because they believe in freedom and justice. (*Coughs.*) And I am here because I wanted the use of a car. They're dying for their country. (*Laughs.*) Because I was vain or frivolous enough to believe it was my right.

PADRE: But you too, have served your country.

IVOR: No, I crashed them. They tried to get me to fly planes – I did nothing. They might as well have fought the war with a cello string.

PADRE: And yet you did more with one song than if you'd flown a thousand times. And those people who heard your song, even those who are fighting right now, they believe in you, Ivor.

IVOR: In my music? In the hope. What is that, when your son is blown apart on a foreign beach? What is hope then?

PADRE: More than either of us can imagine.

IVOR: No, you're wrong. I am nothing.

PADRE: Why are you like this, now? Now, when you are doing so well?

IVOR: Doing well? (*Coughs*.) Ivor Novello. Doing well at doing porridge.

PADRE: But you are, Ivor. The Governor is pleased with you. The inmates like you. You haven't been sick, you've even refused the infirmary. You've done your work, you've been no trouble. You've been an ideal prisoner.

IVOR: An ideal prisoner? What an absurd... an ideal prisoner?!

PADRE: Why absurd?

IVOR: Because the word 'prisoner' means the same thing whichever way you describe it. This is a system that treats the people – whether it is murder, violence, or a simple breach of a war regulation – they treat us all the same, in here. The lowest form of humanity, no matter what their crime. And out there? It's all the same.

PADRE: No, Ivor, it's not. Not out there. And one day it will change in here, too. I can promise you that.

IVOR: Oh hell, I just hate it. I loathe and despise every second of it, and I pray God to let me forget it all. All of it.

PADRE: I don't know if you will be able to forget it. But they will outside, believe me. Look at me Ivor. Now listen, the Governor has received a letter from your press secretary.

IVOR: Oh God, the press. (*Coughs.*)

PADRE: It seems they want you to return to the stage as soon as possible. It seems that the public are already waiting to find out when you will return.

IVOR: What?

PADRE: The letter goes on to say that they will announce your return to the Adelphi as soon as they know the date.

IVOR: But I shan't return.

PADRE: Would you like to see the letter?

IVOR: I can't return.

PADRE: I'll tell you what, now. I'll talk to the Governor, and let you see the letter. Maybe I can even get you some music paper. Music paper, Ivor. So that you can write. Perhaps you could write me a little musical something set in Wales.

IVOR: Music paper?

PADRE: Yes. That should help with the boredom. But as for your state of mind, I cannot really say anything, except things are not as bad as you think they are. Truly, they are not.

Pause.

IVOR: Perhaps now, I should consider disappearing. I could rent a little cottage outside Cardiff and vanish from sight.

PADRE: Could you ever really return to Wales?

IVOR (*looks at the PADRE*): I don't know. My home is the theatre. (*Coughs.*) That's my life.

PADRE: And I think you have more work in you, don't you? I think your head is full of much, much more.

IVOR: The only thing in my head right now is a migraine.

PADRE: Really? Some of the men in here have nothing left but despair. All they need is a little hope. But none of them had so much left to do as you have.

IVOR: I don't understand you.

PADRE: You said it yourself. Theatre is your whole life. Is that why you turned your back on everything else? If it is, then you still have a debt to pay, don't you? You still have so much to write. I couldn't ever really leave the church, and I'm sure it is the same for you.

IVOR: I don't even know if I can leave here. I'm so afraid.

PADRE: Is that so terrible?

IVOR: I think it is. What am I to do when I get out? How do I face them all? And the Press. Oh, the Press.

PADRE: Well, I don't think you should. Not straight away.

IVOR: But they'll be waiting outside for me. I've never known real fear until now, and I'm so afraid. And I'm afraid I should collapse.

PADRE: Yes, but think. Tonight is Saturday night, correct?

IVOR: Yes.

PADRE: But it could really be Sunday morning, for all you know.

IVOR: I don't understand.

PADRE: Well, you are due to go free on Monday, June 12th, aren't you?

IVOR: Yes.

PADRE: Well, I think the photographers will be expecting you in the morning. But technically you are free to go when Monday begins. Which is at midnight. If you could leave then, your friends could take you home then. That way you can spend a few days recovering before you need even think about your public life.

Beat.

IVOR: Do you think that might be possible?

PADRE: We can but request it. The Governor is a good man, I can't see why he'd not grant it. And then you can forget all about the Press.

IVOR: But Padre, I will be able to forget all this, won't I? I don't mean the suffering of the others in here, I always want to be aware of that. Yes, I should always like to be aware of that. Of them. (*Coughs.*) But how long is it going to take me to forget this? Not what has happened, no – what I mean is, my actual feelings? How I feel right now. Will I ever forget that?

Ivor's music plays softly in the background.

PADRE: I don't know, Ivor. How long does it take to forget a thing, an event, a life? I don't know.

A light comes up on the LEADING LADY. For a while, as she sings, they are still talking, dimly lit. Eventually the lights on the cell fade. The PADRE leaves, and IVOR lies down.

LADY (*sings*): 'I can give you the mountains
　　　　　　　Pools of shimmering blue
　　　　　　　Call and I shall be
　　　　　　　All you ask of me
　　　　　　　Music in spring, flowers for a king
　　　　　　　All these I bring to you.'

Scene Seven

Prison Cell No. 242, Wormwood Scrubs.

MAM: Ivor, Ivor. Wake up.

IVOR: Mamsie.

MAM: I'm here.

IVOR: Yes, I can see that. But why are you here? I'm not going mad anymore. Everything is fine, now. You needn't be here.

MAM: Oh, Ivor, would you listen to yourself. Of course you're not going mad. I see you're eating a little porridge, now, that's good.

IVOR: Yes, Mam.

MAM: Of course you're wrong about your father. He may have been quiet, but he could put his foot down, when he needed to.

IVOR: Why are you here Mam?

MAM: He could you know. When we were courting, I was never too sure that he was the man for me. We had an understanding, true, but there were other young men after the heart of Clara Davies. So one day, for no apparent reason, he hailed a cab, bundled me in and told the owner to keep driving until he was told to stop. 'Now Clara,' he said, 'we're going to have it over and done with once and for all. Either you marry me four weeks from now, or not at all. Make your mind up.'

IVOR: 'And don't forget this cab costs money.'

MAM: Sure enough, four weeks later, I walked down the aisle: a lace veil with orange blossoms on it, a dress of cream brocade satin, and a bouquet of lilies of the valley. You see, he could stand up for himself, when he needed to.

IVOR: But he never did, Mam. Not after that.

MAM: Well that's because he knew I was always right. He believed in me. Unlike my own son.

IVOR: What?

MAM: I could have done wonderful things with my life if it wasn't for you always getting in the way.

IVOR: That is a horrid thing to say.

MAM: At least I had your music. At least the world will remember me through you. I believe you to have been my greatest creation. And I am thankful that I have put you where you are.

IVOR: Mam, you didn't put me anywhere. You didn't make me who I am. If it were up to you I would never have gone into the theatre. You sabotaged my first job.

MAM: A chorus part at Daly's? Fate sabotaged that. Destiny was not going to sit by and watch you ruin your life.

IVOR: But quite happy to watch thousands of pounds go down the drain on account of some scheme of yours? Some ridiculous scheme I had to save you from.

MAM: I won't talk to you when you are like this.

IVOR: Oh, Mam, I have devoted my life to you. And if that meant saving you occasionally, then I did it gladly.

MAM: Saving me. I could have conquered America if you'd had a little more faith in me. I could have.

IVOR: You were broke in New York. I sent you money to pay the debt.

MAM: And forced me to come home. If you'd just given me a little more money. But no, as ever I was your last consideration.

IVOR: My last? No, always my first.

MAM: You tried to rule me, Ivor. And no one has ever ruled me, certainly not my only son.

IVOR: I could never rule you. I tried once and you took to your bed for three days and told us all that it was the end. Three whole days. I was so worried about you I paid all your debts just to make sure you'd eat something.

MAM: You saw that I was right in the end, you see.

IVOR: Mam, you know there is nothing I wouldn't do for you.

MAM: I should think so, too. But then I have always been there for you. Do you remember the trip across the Atlantic. When we got the wire to offer you that film part. I'm so glad I made you take it.

IVOR: Mam, I think you are mistaken. Bobbie was the one who said I should take that offer.

MAM: Bobbie. Rubbish. Bobbie's not a mother. Not a wife. What has Bobbie ever done?

IVOR: Don't talk like that. Don't ever talk about Bobbie like that.

MAM: After everything I have done for you? I sent off for that Oxford scholarship. I did that. I created that. I gave birth to you and I've steered you to where you are now, and you know it.

IVOR: Well, then if it wasn't for you I wouldn't be here right now. In this prison.

MAM: What a ridiculous notion. You are here because of your own foolish behaviour.

IVOR: And who taught me that behaviour, Mam? Who taught me to live in this illusion that I think is life? To be proud and vain? To feel I deserve anything I want, that I can conquer any obstacle? You. So, then, why I am in this hell right now? Because you never taught me otherwise. That's why.

MAM: I didn't raise a son of mine to talk to me like that. You take that back this instant, David Ivor Davies, you take that back.

IVOR: No, I won't. It's Ivor Novello, and I created that. If I didn't, if you're so sure that you created me, then you have to take responsibility for this, too.

MAM: I will not be spoken to like that. I'm warning you, Ivor, you take that back, or I'll walk out that door and I'll not speak to you ever again.

IVOR: Don't play the *grande-dame* with me. You know it doesn't work.

MAM: I mean it, my boy. I'll walk.

Pause. IVOR laughs.

IVOR: Oh, Mamsie, the last time you tried to walk out on me, you stormed straight into a broom closet.

MAM: And you laughed at me then.

IVOR: And so I am now.

MAM: And I hate and love you for it as much now as I did then.

Beat.

IVOR: Mam, could you ever foresee me, here? In all your dreams, however crazed, did this place ever picture as a place for me?

MAM: In all my dreams? (*Thinks.*) I always knew you'd be a boy. Just as I had known your sister would be a girl. And perhaps her death brought me closer to you, I don't know. But I knew you must be a boy. How I wished for a boy; a beautiful baby boy with music in his soul. You were made to order, Ivor. A beautiful, talented boy. I wanted so much for you. But most of all, I wanted music for you. Do you know, you even cried in perfect thirds, even in your wailing you made music. My boy. David Ivor Davies. How I dreamt of you at the opera house, conducting the music that flowed from me to you, through those months of joy. But, despite all those dreams, years of happiness are what you have brought me. Such a beautiful nature, such a wonderful child. And a child you are still, darling; a misguided, foolish, but, oh so wonderful, child.

IVOR: Mam, I'm so sorry. So sorry I never brought your grandchildren into the world. How I would love a family of my own. How I adore children, Mam. But instead I've brought you nothing, more than this. This shame.

MAM: Ivor, my ridiculous, soft boy. A lifetime of grandchildren would be as nothing without you. We are each other, as I am you, so you are me. Nothing you could do would disappoint me. I could feel nothing but pride for you. I only wish I could spare you from this present... this present imperfect. Turn you into song and let you float out into the world once more. Save you as you so often saved me.

IVOR: Hold me, Mam.

MAM: Always. Just here. (*She starts to leave, but, stopping at the door, she turns. The music for* My Dearest Dear *is heard.*) Always. (*She goes.*)

IVOR: Goodbye, Mam.

LADY (*sings*): 'You'd understand
    How slight the shadow that is keeping us apart
    So take my hand
    I'll lead the way for you
    A little waiting and you'll reach my heart.'

Scene Eight

Prison Cell No. 242, Wormwood Scrubs.

June 11th. It is the evening of IVOR's departure. The PADRE stands at the cell door.

PADRE: So, Ivor, it's time for goodbye.

IVOR: Yes, I believe it is.

PADRE: You'll be all right until midnight?

IVOR: They are taking me home, Padre, I'll be just marvellous.

PADRE: And you will come and visit us?

IVOR: No, I think not. I would very much like to do what I can, to send some of my company to visit, to entertain the men here. I would like very much to do that for them. But I don't think I could return.

PADRE: No.

IVOR (*coughs*): Although Frankie told me that the next time I need some petrol, I was simply to go to him.

They laugh.

Beat.

PADRE: I shouldn't say it's been a pleasure, but it has.

IVOR: No, you shouldn't say, no. It has been a bit of a nightmare for me.

PADRE: You've coped admirably well, though. See, I knew you would.

IVOR: Yes, I suppose I have, Duckie. And I do hope you and your wife will be my guest if I decide to return to the stage.

PADRE: I'm sure my wife will be as honoured as I.

IVOR: One thing though.

PADRE: Yes.

IVOR: Well, it's bit of a disappointment, really.

PADRE: And what's that?

IVOR: Well, I have always been surrounded by people you see. I've never been alone. Not like this.

PADRE: And...

IVOR: It seems silly now, but I suppose I had this rather naive notion that I should 'find myself', if I were alone, I mean.

PADRE: Find yourself?

IVOR: Yes. Discover something about myself.

PADRE: Like what?

IVOR: I don't know. Some rare new philosophy. (*Coughs.*) A revelation, perhaps? Something, I don't know.

PADRE: And you haven't?

IVOR: No, I fear not at all. I feel like I've learned nothing.

PADRE: Are you angry about that?

IVOR: I'm angry about something. And yet powerless to vent that, also. Who am I angry at? Who am I resentful of? I'm not sure. Certainly not my fans. And yet they're the ones I fear most now.

PADRE: Do you not think they'll be there for you?

IVOR: How can I expect them to be there for me? Really?

PADRE: I think it always best not to expect anything, don't you? Not from anyone, not even one's self.

Beat.

IVOR: Perhaps – and it is possible that, when I get home, all this suffering and loneliness will do something for me in the long run.

PADRE: I'm certain of it.

The PADRE shakes IVOR's hand.

PADRE: And I look forward to a show about the homeland.

IVOR: Yes. Daffodil Dilys, or something?

The PADRE laughs.

IVOR: Thank you for everything you've done for me.

PADRE: My pleasure.

The LEADING LADY enters the cell.

PADRE: Good luck, Mr Ivor. Good Luck. (*He exits.*)

LADY (*sings* Waltz of My Heart):
>'Waltz of my heart
>Haunting and gay
>Calling enthrallingly
>Waltzing away
>
>Ring out your bells for me, ivory keys
>Weave out your spell for me, orchestra, please!
>Chorus of wings, thrilling the sky
>While you're inspiring me, time hurries by
>Joy fans a fire in me, soon as you start
>Sweeping your strings, waltz of my heart
>
>The lark is singing on high
>The sun's ashine in the blue
>The winter is driven away
>And spring is returning anew
>Who cares what sorrow may bring?
>What storms may tear us apart?
>No sadness can kill the wonder and thrill
>Of that waltz in my heart.'

Scene Nine

The Adelphi, off-stage.

June 20th, 1944.

BOBBIE (*entering*): Ivor? Ivor?

LADY: Where is he?

BOBBIE: He was in his dressing room just a moment ago.

LADY: How long ago?

BOBBIE: No more than five minutes.

LADY: Are you sure you left him in here?

BOBBIE: No, I left him in the car – he's not a little dog, M.

LADY: Do you think he's all right?

BOBBIE: I don't know, I thought we were over the worst.

LADY: Do you think tonight's a mistake? Too soon?

BOBBIE: I think we shall soon find out.

LADY: I'll go and tell someone. (*She exits.*)

BOBBIE: Ivor?

IVOR (*off*): Do you know, I do adore this theatre, it's just my cup of tea, just the right size. (*Enters in a dressing gown.*) I hope I stop here a long time, I think I even prefer it to the Lane.

BOBBIE: Why didn't you answer me? Just now, when I called?

IVOR: One thing I've always been able to do, darling, is to create a stir. (*Smiles.*) Now, I was thinking I might have a little nap before the show.

99

BOBBIE: You can't take a nap, Ivor, and I don't think this is very funny. Time's ticking away; you simply have to get ready.

IVOR: As a matter of fact, I don't have to do anything. I can do what I like.

BOBBIE: I beg your pardon, Mr Novello. You have a show to do.

IVOR: And if I decide not to do the show, Mr Andrews, what will you do? Will you go on in my stead? What does one do, if Mr Novello decides to walk out that door. You see that door, Bobbie? I believe you can. That door is not locked. No. I can open that door and go out. No door is locked anymore, I can go through any of them freely. I can open windows. I am free: I can go anywhere and I can do whatever I like.

Pause.

BOBBIE: I know.

Beat.

BOBBIE: We all can, when you think about it.

IVOR: And if I decided not to, what would you do? If I decided to go for a walk and then a little supper at the Ivy, what would you do then?

BOBBIE: You know I'm very partial to the Ivy.

IVOR (*smiles*): Why?

100

BOBBIE: Because it's so close to where we live.

IVOR: No, not that, no. Why are you still here?

BOBBIE: Why am I still here?

IVOR: While you were panicking about my whereabouts, I was in there, thinking about when I first met you.

BOBBIE: January 1917, the Strand Theatre.

IVOR: And do you still remember the play?

BOBBIE: *Under Cover*. Starring Margaret Bannerman.

Beat.

IVOR: Well?

BOBBIE: Well, Ivor, why are you still with me?

Beat.

BOBBIE: Eh?

BOY (*popping his head around the corner*): I'm sorry to...

BOBBIE: Ivor's busy right now.

IVOR: No, no, Bobbie, let him be. What is it, Eddie?

BOY: I just wanted to say break a leg for tonight.

IVOR: Thank you.

BOY: And, well, if its not too much trouble, would you sign a playbill for my mother.

IVOR: Your mother?

BOY: Yes, I told her you were coming back and so she decided to come to town and welcome you home.

IVOR: Where does she live?

BOY: I don't think that would have mattered, really.

Pause.

IVOR: Oh, dear boy, of course I'll sign it. Come and see me in the interval.

BOY: Thank you, Ivor.

IVOR: Now you'd better go.

BOY: Yes, of course. Thank you, Ivor. I'm so sorry to have disturbed.

IVOR: It's quite all right.

The BOY stalls a second longer.

IVOR: What is it?

BOY: I'll try and make sure you're on the mantelpiece, this time.

IVOR (*laughs*): Dear, sweet boy. Thank you.

BOY: Always. (*He leaves.*)

IVOR takes BOBBIE's arm.

IVOR: Mr Andrews, I think this whole sordid little episode, this little illusion that took place in cell no. 242, I think it is best forgotten now, don't you?

BOBBIE: I couldn't agree more.

IVOR: In which case, no official statements, no interviews, promise me that.

BOBBIE nods.

IVOR: In fact, I should prefer...

Beat.

IVOR: If we simply never mentioned it again.

BOBBIE: I don't even know what you're talking about, Mr Novello.

Beat.

BOBBIE: Shall we?

BOBBIE leads IVOR off stage. The applause swells and there is a spotlight on IVOR.

Scene Ten

The Adelphi, on-stage.

June 20th, 1944.

IVOR: Mam, Mam, are you out there? No? There. There you are. That's where I'd have placed you, Mam. Just there. Funny, you'd seem a lot closer than you did at the Lane. Oh, but I'm so sorry, how thoughtless of me, but with all this fuss, I forgot to put out your flowers. How you love showing off those flowers.

Showing off. Listen to them. Would you be proud of me, now? Listen to them. They're still going, they're still applauding. What a night tonight has been.

What a strange night, tonight. The auditorium packed, like a first night almost, hardly more than a handful of latecomers. The sirens were calling outside but the tension inside, Mam, the suspense inside the auditorium. I felt as if I were going out there for the first time all over again. And then, just before my entrance, a flying bomb landed, somewhere not too far away, like a forewarner of some catastrophic disaster. And then it was time.

When I walked on stage tonight, I smiled at them, Mam. I suddenly remembered sharing the stage with Sybil Vane, all those many moons ago, and I smiled. Do you remember? When we played them that little money-spinner, all those years ago? How they joined in? Nine times we had to sing it for them. Astonishing. And tonight it was the same. They wouldn't stop. They just kept applauding. And then, when I turned to start that first scene, they sounded the all-clear. Outside. Funny, the streets of London became silent once again, just so some little *divertissement* of mine could continue uninterrupted.

104

And now they're applauding again. Good God, I think some of them are trying to sing. They're weeping, Mam. What is all this nonsense, now? It's not as if I'd won the VC. I only did a little time.

Just a month. What's a month? I've got the rest of my life. I think I've got a few more shows in me yet. I can feel the old blood working again. The muse feeding it. It is a fickle old thing, that muse. You know, I've got an idea for a show set in Wales, Mam. That should please you. I thought I might call it *Lily of the Valley*. About time too, you say. Yes, well, I wonder what they'll make of it back home. I wonder if they even think of me as Welsh. I wonder how much longer it will be before this all ends. I do so hope I'm gone before then.

Doubt? No, not doubt, Mam, no. Just a little tune of music that runs under the main melody. I was a little afraid tonight, though, if truth be told. That little scene after the Nazis. That scene with Maria Zeigler. When she comes to him, you know, afterwards.... I was most afraid of that scene.

MAM: The bullies are getting stronger, Rudi.

IVOR: Not Rudi. Not Rudi, no. Every day.

MAM: The bullies are getting stronger everyday.

IVOR: That's the scene, Mam.

MAM: Turning our whole world upside down.

IVOR: All the more reason for me to carry on resisting them. I don't mind the danger. Even when they locked me up, I didn't mind – my thoughts were far away, somewhere with you – back over the years. *The Dancing Years* – some happy, some sad, but all so full of wonderful memories.

MAM: For both of us. They'll come again. And you know what they will say...

LEADING LADY (*sings*): 'No sadness can kill
                                    The wonder and thrill...'

IVOR: What will they say, Mam?

MAM (*speaks as the LEADING LADY sings her last line*): You made the whole world dance.

LEADING LADY (*sings*): 'Of that waltz in my heart.'

A spotlight on the PADRE. He is, in effect, still in the cell, the evening Ivor was released.

PADRE (*repeats his last line*): Good luck Mr Ivor. Good luck.

Fade to black.

The End.

SEX
AND POWER
AT THE
BEAU RIVAGE

LEWIS DAVIES

Sex and Power at the Beau Rivage was first produced by Theatr Y Byd at the Sherman Theatre, Cardiff, on the 19th March 2003.

Cast:

D H Lawrence	–	Brendan Charleson
Rhys Davies	–	Morgan Rhys
Frieda Lawrence	–	Martina Messing

Creative Team:

Director	–	Chris Morgan
Designer	–	James North
Production Manager	–	Dave Roxborough
Stage Manager	–	Jim Mayer

ACT ONE

A man walks to the foot of the steps that lead up to the hotel. He is dressed in a suit, wears a stiff hat and carries a small travelling case. He stands out as an Englishman abroad. He looks up at the terrace. Light comes through the shutters. He is a little nervous that he is really where he is.

A man enters the dining room. He is shouting back, further into the hotel.

LAWRENCE: Yes, today, of course it is today. Today is *Samedi*. He will come on Saturday, he said. I do not care what you think. I will tell him he can't wait.

The conversation fades out. LAWRENCE checks the dining room then crosses to the terrace. He wears a faded, blue blazer; wispy, cotton trousers; a black hat/beret. He does not look English. He has a love of life that marches before him. As he comes through the terrace, he sees the visitor.

LAWRENCE: Ah, Mr Davies. We are so glad you could come. You do not know what it means for us to have visitors.

RHYS: A pleasure, it is so er... unexpected.

LAWRENCE: I like to meet people who write, don't you?

RHYS: I hadn't realised you had read my work.

LAWRENCE: Oh, I read lots of things, Mr Davies, people are always sending me things in brown envelopes.

RHYS: It is such a pleasure to have invitations. From such people as yourselves.

LAWRENCE: The pleasure is ours.

Beat.

LAWRENCE: And such a journey. All the way from Nice.

RHYS: Really, it is not that far.

LAWRENCE: And you travel so lightly. You cannot rely on porters in a place like this.

RHYS: I don't find I need much.

LAWRENCE: No, of course. It is better that way – always light and open to suggestions. My wife will be so glad to see you. She will be here now. She is never quite ready for guests.

RHYS: Were you able to secure me a room?

LAWRENCE: Of course, now that the season is finished it is no problem. I find the resort much better without the French in it. They're terrible – restricted, you know.

RHYS: I am getting used to them.

LAWRENCE: Of course, of course. I treat you as a boy out of school, not a man who has had such a fine first book published. I'm so glad you responded.

RHYS: It was a honour to be asked. A shock, actually.

LAWRENCE: Oh, I like to keep people amused and if I can't do that, I'll frighten them. It is such a fine thing that you can be here. She will be so pleased. You haven't met my wife of course but you soon will. I expect you've heard all sorts of the most outrageous things about her but she is really perfectly charming.

RHYS: I'm looking forward to it.

LAWRENCE: I can see she will like you straight away. She's read your book too. She was charmed by it. And then to find you are staying just along the coast from us. What a stroke of fine luck.

RHYS: Yes....

LAWRENCE: And the coast here is wonderful, don't you think? Spring is here and it is still February. The mimosa will be flowering soon. It is such an effusive plant I can't but warm to it. The lizards, too. I caught one on the terrace yesterday. Funny things they are, a million years old and still on the same coast as they were when this place was young without any of us. I looked into its eye and I could see eternity.

RHYS: Is the hotel... one of the... I need to know the... (*he is nervous about cost*).

LAWRENCE: It is not expensive in the least. And it's of no matter. You are to be our guest. We such enjoy having people here.

RHYS: It is very generous of you.

LAWRENCE: Ah, money. It always comes, you know.

RHYS: I'm still trying to believe that.

LAWRENCE: Never enough, I'm sure. But you should only spend what you can.

RHYS: I'm not used to staying on the front.

LAWRENCE: We must be right on the *plage*. The sun comes up over the water in the morning. It is so bright here, the light fills me with a hope I haven't had for years. But let not an old man tell you his follies. We must meet the duchess.

They climb the hotel terrace. There is no sign of FRIEDA.

LAWRENCE: She will be here now. Frieda? I can't think where she has got to. Frieda? Frieda? (*Turning to RHYS:*) perhaps you can take a seat. I will just ask the the proprietor. He will need to see you, anyway. Are you alright here, for a few moments? Of course you are. A man of the world. You're at home anywhere. I will return shortly with my prize.

RHYS is alone. He surveys the terrace, sits in a chair, closes his eyes against the sun. FRIEDA enters. RHYS doesn't hear. She sneaks up behind him and puts her hands over his eyes. He gets up quickly, startled and embarrassed. FRIEDA is rather pleased with her joke.

FRIEDA: Mr Davies, you mustn't be alarmed.

RHYS: I'm sorry. You startled me.

FRIEDA: It is only natural. I enjoy the unexpected, Mr Davies.

RHYS: Please, call me 'Rhys'. My father is 'Mr Davies'.

FRIEDA: I wouldn't want to get you mixed up.

RHYS: Most certainly.

FRIEDA: I'm sure he is a man of charm. Most of the fathers I've known are. Except Lawrence's. He was an uncouth pig.

RHYS: Relations can be difficult.

FRIEDA: You were lucky not to meet him. What he thought of me he made plain: 'When 'er oppens 'er mahth 'aif room's dark.' I didn't mind the plain speaking, it was the accent.

RHYS: I'm afraid I never had much of an accent.

FRIEDA: Nonsense, Mr Davies, we are defined by our voices. I was thrown out of Cornwall on account of sounding German. They thought I was feeding the submarines. What with, I have no idea.

RHYS: I think London has done for mine. There are so many different voices, it doesn't matter.

FRIEDA: It always matters. Lawrence says they are unimportant. It doesn't matter to him. But I tell him the rest of the world is not built on the sensibilities of D H Lawrence.

LAWRENCE returns, as FRIEDA finishes her sentence.

LAWRENCE: It should be. Then we could all live together in peace and harmony and democracy – as long as they listen to me. Mr Davies, I see you have met my wife.

FRIEDA: He insists I call him 'Rhys'.

LAWRENCE: On first name terms already. You always have been forward.

FRIEDA: I try to keep within the bounds of decency.

LAWRENCE: I'm sure you shall. But what will Mr Davies think of that?

RHYS: 'Rhys', if you can. I find it easier to listen.

LAWRENCE: Of course. 'Rhys' it shall be. A fine name. You are one of the few to reply to my letters. And to accept an invitation. No one seems to be replying to this curious place. It's as if we're in Mexico again.

RHYS: I find the mail in Nice excellent.

LAWRENCE: It must be me then.

RHYS: I didn't mean that...

FRIEDA: All the way from Nice. Such a fine journey you made to be with us in this hotel by the sea.

RHYS: The journey was nothing, really. *Bon journaie*, as they say.

LAWRENCE: He's even picked up a bit of French.

RHYS: I try.

LAWRENCE: A long way from the valley, now.

RHYS: I find myself there every afternoon.

LAWRENCE: Working on a new novel, I hear.

RHYS: Yes, the reason for Nice.

LAWRENCE: And is it going well?

RHYS: I work at it. It will mend itself maybe, if I push on.

LAWRENCE: Work – that is the only thing for a writer.

RHYS: Are you able to work here?

LAWRENCE: I am writing some poems.

RHYS: I have not read much of your poetry.

LAWRENCE: Nor me. I find it easier that way – on everyone.

RHYS: Have they been suppressed?

LAWRENCE: For a long time. My life is the same. I try to live it for myself but the gods won't let me. Just now they let me paint.

On the terrace there are a number of large, expressive canvases, based on nude figures.

RHYS: They are quite, er, exuberant.

LAWRENCE: Frieda, we have an art critic. Sign him up for *The Squib* immediately.

RHYS: *The Squib*?

LAWRENCE: Yes, it's a new magazine I'm going to be editing. But it must be published in London. I'm looking for some writers with passion.

RHYS: I'm sure I might be able to find something.

LAWRENCE: That's no good. You've got to force it on them. They'll scream but it'll be good for them in the end. What do you say?

RHYS: Will it be medicine or writing?

LAWRENCE: Both. You shed your sickness in books.

FRIEDA: Stop teasing our guest. (*She walks over and stands next to one of the canvases, which clearly shows her naked.*) It is a fine likeness, don't you think?

RHYS walks up to FRIEDA and her nude image, but doesn't reply directly.

LAWRENCE: You don't like them?

RHYS: I've never seen anything like them.

LAWRENCE: Of course, they're mine.

RHYS: They capture form.

LAWRENCE: Some people believe there is nothing beneath our clothes. No cocks or cunts.

RHYS: There's certainly... revelation.

LAWRENCE: It is only flesh.

RHYS: The form is striking.

LAWRENCE: I'm not the first to paint in the flesh.

RHYS: No, but it still frightens people.

LAWRENCE: It shouldn't. The boys on the beach, do you see them ashamed of what hangs between their legs?

RHYS: The English seem to want some decorum.

LAWRENCE: They are told what flesh is and now they are confusing dirt with sex. Sex is to be enjoyed. It is part of life.

RHYS: But part of our lives are hidden.

LAWRENCE: By hiding from life we become afraid of it. Just now, people are afraid of me. Do I frighten you, Mr Davies?

RHYS: I have my reservations.

LAWRENCE: They will be no good to you here. My wife and I have no reservations.

FRIEDA: Lawrence, you are preaching again. Let Rhys have his say. He is not on a lecture tour.

LAWRENCE: Well?

RHYS: I am not used to the directness of what you are showing me.

LAWRENCE: What I am trying to do is a celebration of it. I cannot help the colours and tone, the light here is wonderful for colours, it goes deep into your blood. You must have sensed it.

RHYS: I find life is a lot easier in the south.

LAWRENCE: Yes, that's it. You have understood. Men do not toil for the sun here, it surrounds them.

RHYS: People can be blinded by too much light.

LAWRENCE: You should see Australia – there is a country blinded by the vastness of its light. Here, I feel the peasants have found their way through to it. Eat well, drink well and get up at ten o'clock in the morning. I bet there is nothing like this in Wales.

RHYS: We have seasons and chapels.

LAWRENCE: And coal – that is our connection. We must open a bottle of wine to mark it. A fine rosé filled with the sun of Provence.

FRIEDA opens a bottle of wine. She pours out three glasses.

LAWRENCE: To new friends and Americans. The only people who answer my letters.

RHYS: To new friends.

They drink.

LAWRENCE: Did you know there's a new print of my book in New York?

RHYS: I thought your American publisher had been unable to print *Lady Chatterley*?

LAWRENCE: He is well informed, Frieda. A young man who reads.

RHYS: Charles mentioned it to me.

LAWRENCE: I didn't know about his one. Apparently, they are so popular I am printed as a copy. I can't sell my own edition and a man in New York is asking twenty-five pounds for *Lady Chatterley's Lover* and I will not see a penny.

RHYS: Isn't it illegal?

LAWRENCE: Of course it is. But I am here in Europe, thousands of miles away. What does he care?

RHYS: We should do something.

LAWRENCE: Frieda, a new hero to my defence.

RHYS: There is no need to laugh.

LAWRENCE: Of course not, but, you see, to be copied is a success of sorts. Every writer must strive to be plagiarised.

RHYS: You cannot sue him?

LAWRENCE: Of course not. Then I will robbed by lawyers instead of publishers.

RHYS: What will you do?

LAWRENCE: When I meet the man I shall ask him for his response and then refuse the money he offers.

RHYS: Why?

LAWRENCE: He will die regretting his debt.

RHYS: But what of now?

LAWRENCE: I should get another edition privately printed. It is enough to cut the profit they can make. For the money I do not care but I do need something on which to live. But enough of my problems. Tell me of mutual friends. It was Charles that sent me your book. Does he still search the barrows of Charing Cross Road?

RHYS: Every morning.

LAWRENCE: In shorts and sandals?

RHYS: Trousers after November, but no socks, even in the snow.

LAWRENCE: Tell me, has he been good to you?

RHYS: The best – he lets me have books to read and forced my first stories into print.

LAWRENCE: For a bookseller he is a fine man. Not like publishers, they will rot in hell. A special hell just for them.

RHYS: Are there others who might publish your work?

LAWRENCE: *Lady Chatterley?* No one. They are afraid of of it. There are always conditions. They want me to take out the swear words. Imagine an English publisher scared of printing four letters. They cannot take the risk. Printers are a different breed. They will risk anything for money.

RHYS: Charles lent me a copy.

LAWRENCE: Another loss of royalty.

RHYS: I'm sorry... I...

LAWRENCE: Frieda, he takes everything I say seriously. Tell him to stop it or we'll cancel the oysters.

FRIEDA: You must allow Lawrence his jokes.

LAWRENCE: I am not the ogre of popular repute. I have a sense of humour.

FRIEDA: Perhaps Rhys is having a difficulty in locating your humours.

LAWRENCE: Very good, *fraulein*. Are you leaving us now?

FRIEDA: I thought I would stay. It is rude to leave our new guest so early.

RHYS: Oh I don't mind. I mean, if you want to that is?

FRIEDA: I want nothing of importance just now.

LAWRENCE: Now she is teasing you, Rhys. You must excuse. She fears being misunderstood.

RHYS: It is a nature of the human condition.

LAWRENCE: That is why we write. To portray to the world, *this is what I meant. This is my idea*, however wrong you think I am.

FRIEDA: And are your words believed?

LAWRENCE: They all think I am a liar. I show them how the world is and I am reviled for it.

RHYS: As a writer, I fear I have become an outsider.

LAWRENCE: You could be nothing else. But there is a danger to it. Remain outside too long and you will become cold. There will be nothing to write about but the grey embers of your childhood.

FRIEDA: Do not frighten him with your age, Lawrence. Rhys looks like he's still in the first run of youth.

LAWRENCE: I think he is maturing well.

RHYS: Ripening in sun?

LAWRENCE: I hope your next book is better than that.

RHYS: I'm afraid just now it isn't.

LAWRENCE: As you said, work. And the kitchen have been working for us. We must eat early here. The staff do not like to work later than three. They don't start until ten, finish at three. Then come in again at six, if the sun hasn't got the better of them. What a country. Are you hungry?

RHYS: No, not yet.

FRIEDA: It is still an hour before dinner is served.

LAWRENCE: Then a cocktail. I will send someone with drinks. There must be someone in the place. If not I shall mix them myself.

FRIEDA: He makes the most wonderful rum bumba's, would you like one?

RHYS: Do you have any gin?

LAWRENCE: Of course, I will send the waiter.

RHYS: Are you not going to join us?

LAWRENCE: There are more letters I must write. Frieda's mother likes us to keep her informed. And Frieda is not so good at writing the letters.

FRIEDA: He mocks my written German, but come, Rhys, or the time will go too quickly.

The sounds of the harbour/shorefront surround them.

FRIEDA: It is such fun to watch the boats on the water.

RHYS: I feel as if I watch a different species. They have knowledge of things of which I know nothing.

FRIEDA: But of course. They are in their own world and we in ours. I always find it is a kind of magic that there are so many worlds and yet we all share this, the only one.

RHYS: I am finding it hard leaving mine.

FRIEDA: Are you still missing home?

RHYS: This has been my first Christmas away from Wales.

FRIEDA: I was nineteen when I first went to England. A new bride in a new country. It was so unutterably strange. The coldness of it all.

RHYS: You were not happy there?

FRIEDA: I was young and it was an adventure. Within months I was pregnant. And within a few years I had three children, a house with servants and a husband who loved me.

RHYS: But it didn't last?

FRIEDA: No, nothing lasts. You cannot keep still.

RHYS: I find the coast here strange. It is full of people who have washed up here with no better place to go. They're just flotsam caught in these pretty shallow bays.

FRIEDA: It is sunny and warm, they are happy?

RHYS: But there are no roots?

FRIEDA: Your childhood forms you, Rhys. But you cannot, if you are an artist, live within it. Lawrence is a man of the wider world.

RHYS: Yes, I can see that. He doesn't really look English anymore.

FRIEDA: Yet he loves the country, love and hate for what they are trying to do to him and his work.

RHYS: There is a storm raging over his new book.

FRIEDA: I thought it was never going to see the light. It sat in a chest at our villa in Italy for a year. Then he said, 'Shall I publish it, shall I risk the abuse it will bring me?' But he *had* written it. Once he had written it, he believed in it and it had to come out. All of it.

RHYS: The force of it is unexpected.

FRIEDA: He writes about love, that is all.

RHYS: There is a threat in the words.

FRIEDA: Of course, sex is always dangerous. But it is wonderful too, don't you think?

RHYS: Yes, I'm not used to...

FRIEDA: How we need it? Want it above all else? I hope I don't embarrass you, Mr Davies?

RHYS: No, not at all.

FRIEDA: But I do embarass you?

RHYS: You're honest. I'm not used to it. I have got used to deception.

FRIEDA: You are a writer. You deal in fictions. You will probably lie about us all.

RHYS: Maybe.

FRIEDA: It is in our natures. My husband tells the truth and the whole of England hates him for it. They think he is a pornographer. Do you think he's a pornographer, Mr Davies?

RHYS: There is great beauty in it.

FRIEDA: But you do not like it?

RHYS: I struggled to find the humour in it.

FRIEDA: Really, don't you think the English idea of fucking is ridiculous? All straight, from the front?

RHYS: I wouldn't put it quite that way.

FRIEDA: You should surprise yourself. It happens to all people.

RHYS: I find the book is more a cry, a clarion.

FRIEDA: He wants to change people's lives. That is a real ambition. And they hate him for it.

RHYS: Now you are offended. I didn't mean that. I admire him. He is the best of writers and all of us, the younger men look to him.

FRIEDA: Then you must tell him. He thinks everyone in London hates him.

RHYS: Many people don't understand him.

FRIEDA: I think you have to live with him for that. But don't be mean to him, Rhys. I can see you are a nice man. It is good to have nice men around. Sometimes we are surrounded by charlatans.

RHYS: I am not that.

FRIEDA: No, I don't think you are, Mr Davies, but we are all hiding things from each other.

RHYS: I am trying to be myself.

FRIEDA: It is not easy. I thought I could always live my own freedoms but the world won't let you.

RHYS: You seem to have choices?

FRIEDA: We have very little money but it is desire, not money, which allows us to live. Life is for enjoyment, you know.

RHYS: Depends where you're from.

LAWRENCE (*returning, his mood changed*): There is never anyone in this vile place when you want them. (*He remains standing.*) Where are your drinks? Did the waiter bring the drinks?

FRIEDA: We had some of the rosé.

LAWRENCE: I couldn't find anyone and then they send that awful boy to my room. I can't stand it. I ask for service and they disturb me in my room. In the afternoon. This place is slack, no one cares.

RHYS: Is there anything the matter?

LAWRENCE: Did you see him?

LAWRENCE: He is weak.

RHYS: Who is weak?

FRIEDA: Lawrence has conceived a dislike for our Algerian waiter.

LAWRENCE: The man has no spirit, no passion; he has grown soft. There is no life to him. Where is the passion in his blood? The way he walks suggests a lifetime of weakness.

RHYS: Perhaps he is lame.

LAWRENCE: No... yes. The whole country is that.

RHYS: Surely not on the basis of an Algerian waiter?

LAWRENCE: He lets the French take him for granted. And the French, they take everything for granted. They have already forgotten the sacrifice we made for them.

RHYS: When? What sacrifice?

LAWRENCE: The war.

RHYS: Didn't the French also lose many young men?

LAWRENCE: And what for? So the country could descend into this. They are a slippery and predatory nation. Give me the Germans. They are already preparing for the next war.

RHYS: My friend in Nice says they too are lost.

LAWRENCE: Tell me what he knows about the German youth?

RHYS: He's known a few of them.

LAWRENCE: He's retired to Nice?

RHYS: His family own a vineyard in the Rhine.

LAWRENCE: He's landed gentry, festering in the south.

FRIEDA: What's his name?

RHYS: Friedel.

FRIEDA: No, his second name. We are never informal with people of good standing.

LAWRENCE *(to FRIEDA)*: He can't be of good standing to be spending time with the son of a miner.

FRIEDA: We all have our faults.

RHYS: I don't know his exact details. He's a recovering vegetarian.

FRIEDA: And is he doing well?

RHYS: He's booked into a spiritual centre above the town.

LAWRENCE: Heaven preserve us from the spiritualists.

RHYS: He's very amenable, really. He's been very instructive on the life of such a town.

LAWRENCE: He's taken you to a brothel.

RHYS: It was more of a club with assignations.

LAWRENCE: So your friend is screwing the best of French youth.

RHYS: He too has reservations about the French.

LAWRENCE: France is a country finished. It has become weak. The Germans and British who come here feed on the weakness of spirit.

RHYS: I cannot agree.

LAWRENCE: You do need to. It is surrounding you.

FRIEDA: Lawrence dear, can we order?

LAWRENCE: The people here hate me. They want me removed from here. Killed. I am a criminal to her.

RHYS: I'm sorry, I don't follow.

FRIEDA: There is an old English maid staying at the hotel. Lawrence thinks she cares for him. He is attracted to older women.

LAWRENCE: She would have me killed. (*He is railing to himself. He does not always pay direct attention to what is said to him, in reply. He is arguing with his own demons. He needs an audience, but as an audience. RHYS is yet to understand this. FRIEDA is aware of the game.*)

LAWRENCE: Yesterday, in the reading room, she fluttered around me like a moth, lost, while I was reading the paper... I was reading the paper. She wanted it.

FRIEDA: You are angry with her for having desires and not the spirit to ask for it.

LAWRENCE: All of England is the same.

FRIEDA: You should tell her.

LAWRENCE: She is one of the English flowers who try for a late bloom on the coast. Her youth has gone but not her imagination. She knows who I am. She hates me for it. I watch her sketch in the garden. She sketches the flowers and then colours them in purple and blue. The coast is flowering and she tries to capture it on paper. Eventually I turned to her, 'Do you want this? I am reading it.' She turned away in tears.

FRIEDA: You will excuse me, Mr Davies?

LAWRENCE: Where are you going?

FRIEDA: I will see at the reception. There is no sign of our waiter. You have probably driven him back to North Africa.

RHYS stands, allowing FRIEDA to leave. FRIEDA gets up. LAWRENCE glares at her as she leaves but dares not contradict her.

LAWRENCE: Then I feel like the monster she imagined me to be.

RHYS (*remains standing to match LAWRENCE. He is overwhelmed by the speed of the changes but tries to keep up. He is aware he is now with a very different LAWRENCE*): I'm sure she has her qualities.

LAWRENCE: Yes, of course. We all have our secrets. People, they provoke you into words you never wanted to say.

RHYS: Is that how you feel of your books?

LAWRENCE: I mean every word in them. Every word. I cannot help if the world is not ready for them yet.

RHYS: The younger men, we look to you.

LAWRENCE: No, you must look to yourselves.

RHYS: You are ahead of us.

LAWRENCE: Of course. I have worked at it for twenty years, where should I be if not ahead. I have opened things up for you, that is all.

RHYS: We... realise the sacrifice.

LAWRENCE: Nonsense, it is the only way I can live. The young must live for themselves – burn the old.

RHYS: But not the books?

LAWRENCE: Of course the books, especially the books. Set fire to fools like me. Lead yourself.

RHYS: There are always prophets.

LAWRENCE: Yes, usually lost. Or false and I have seen enough of the wilderness.

RHYS: I find new work the best.

LAWRENCE: There is an opportunity now. But I don't see anyone seizing the chance with writing that has blood in it. Blood of passion.

RHYS: You make it sound necessary for writing?

LAWRENCE: It is nothing to do with books. The young should smash what they see as wrong about our world. Rise up and smash. I see none of it. They are forced into it without a fight.

RHYS: I have just enough fire to keep body and soul together.

LAWRENCE: Take your last book.

RHYS: My first.

LAWRENCE: Yes, it was fine, for a first attempt, but where was the real lust, the wet lust of desire?

RHYS: It was about unfulfilled passion.

LAWRENCE: It certainly was.

RHYS: I'm sorry if you didn't like it.

LAWRENCE: You misunderstand me. You think I am a critic.

RHYS: What else are you, in reading my book?

LAWRENCE: It suggests you are afraid of women.

RHYS: They are another country.

LAWRENCE: But they are not, they are part of us as we are part of them and we must fight our way through an understanding of this. We are two parts of the same. Look at you all. No idea how to handle a woman. You wanted to be treated as women. All equal.

RHYS: Isn't that what your books are about? Freedom?

LAWRENCE: Yes, but we are different. Women now are lost, senseless, vicious, they want to be men. And when they become men they will realise they have been fooled and we'll have to start all over.

RHYS: It is men and women who are striving for this equality?

LAWRENCE: And it is men who have failed women because they don't know how to treat them.

RHYS: I'm not sure I follow you directly.

LAWRENCE: No, it will come.

RHYS: Perhaps I will find more with my second.

LAWRENCE: I liked your book for it's promise, it's real attempt to connect with the life that surrounds you.

RHYS: I grew up with it.

LAWRENCE: The Welsh need to take a grip on that part of their magic. The magic that rises with the moon deep in your soul.

RHYS: You make us sound like a nation of mystics.

LAWRENCE: It is the same with the Irish.

RHYS: But they are one nation.

LAWRENCE: And you are not?

RHYS: We are not English, but I fear we do not know what Wales is either.

LAWRENCE: A nation is a country united by an ignorance about its ancestry and a shared hatred of its neighbours.

RHYS: We are our neighbours.

LAWRENCE: Then you are set fair for confusion.

RHYS: I think there may be a few storms.

LAWRENCE: What about your language?

RHYS: It is English.

LAWRENCE: The other one.

RHYS: It is a rare and beautiful orchid brought out for the family on special occasions.

LAWRENCE: So you have a passion, a self-hatred.

RHYS: I am not to be deluded by our faults. I am not blind, it is a wonderful country, once you leave it.

LAWRENCE: And now you have?

RHYS: I had no choice.

LAWRENCE: As a writer, you are always leaving the places that you love.

RHYS: I hated it.

LAWRENCE: For you, I think they are close.

RHYS: I have not had the chance to find out yet.

LAWRENCE: Do you hate the thing you have become?

RHYS: No, I have no choice. The life in Nice, it gives me certain freedoms to enjoy it. They are accepting here. There are many faults in people.

LAWRENCE: And the young man in your novel, is he you?

RHYS: No, I had to use my imagination to create him.

LAWRENCE: That is a very dangerous thing in a writer. You use yourself and become yourself in the minds of others.

RHYS: Surely you can become someone else in your imagination?

LAWRENCE: No, never. You can sleep with someone else. You may find some truth in what you are writing about.

That I think is the most you can hope for as a writer, to find truth in yourself and others.

RHYS: I thought you had to entertain?

LAWRENCE: We are not travelling clowns. Well, not clowns, anyway. Yes, okay, clowns perhaps but then clowns can tell the truth and get away with it. That's what they are frightened of with my work, the truth. The truth might free people.

RHYS: I think the Russians are finding a different truth without their czars.

LAWRENCE: Yes, surely kill your false gods, a few dead royals. Who is the impostor we have in England? And his debauched son pissing away money in that town along the coast. He is as dead as the rest.

RHYS: They say he meets Russian relatives serving his dinner in the hotels.

LAWRENCE: I hope he tips them outrageously.

RHYS: Are you against them?

LAWRENCE: Of course. They keep people down but I cannot be fighting wars over the succession of German princes. They are a dead, soulless people who will bring much misery to the country. But the people, in their foolishness, love them.

RHYS: There are communists in the Rhondda. It might come.

LAWRENCE: The Welsh will cheer the king who starves their children before fighting.

RHYS: You don't believe in a revolution then?

LAWRENCE: Yes, of course, but of the mind not the state. With a revolution of the mind the state becomes obsolete. The Russians fought and they have their new rulers, men who try to impose uniformity on a people. A good honest people who threw off one lot only to find another bunch of tyrants already strapped to their back. They took off their masks as soon as they were in power.

RHYS: The communists talk of freedom for all people.

LAWRENCE: It is easy to talk of it when you have none. It's when you arrive and how you use it, that is important.

RHYS: I think the people will tire of this exploitation.

LAWRENCE: I feel sorry for the Russians all their troubles and revolutions and they will descend to a grubby cheapness, their new god will be materialism.

RHYS: There must be another future for us?

LAWRENCE: Maybe. I have hope when the young have ideals. But you like me are not made to fight among the people, Rhys – you have removed yourself from the mass. How many miners do you see on the coast?

RHYS: The men of the soviet are building new resorts on the Black Sea.

LAWRENCE: And they will be full of party members.

RHYS: I can only write as I see it.

LAWRENCE: Then what's going wrong with your new book?

RHYS: I'm not sure. I feel it is old ground that I am digging over with prospects of nothing but wireworms and nettle stings. There is a mother and daughter in the *pensionne* I am staying. They seem to be from nowhere. Just living here. I give the little girl piano lessons. I am just someone to talk to for a few months. She seems to have no life apart from her mother. She does not go to school and they read books to each other at night. That is no life for a child.

LAWRENCE: You have to take these friendships where they happen.

RHYS: But I fear I am becoming like them.

LAWRENCE: You are trying to understand them, that is all.

RHYS: The loss of it all scares me.

LAWRENCE: The people talk here of the malaise of life. The long afternoons when everything and nothing is perfect. That is when they kill themselves.

RHYS: I try to keep the afternoons free.

LAWRENCE: People retreat into themselves. It is no good for the imagination. You have to go out with the people. Be part of the great mass.

RHYS: Didn't your friend Katherine Mansfield live here?

LAWRENCE: She filled the place with her rancorous presence but now even I cannot smell her.

FRIEDA (*returning to the terrace*): You should be aware of how he talks about his friends.

RHYS: I will keep it in mind.

LAWRENCE: Ignore my wife.

FRIEDA: Despite what he says.

RHYS: I thought her memoirs were very moving. She knew she was dying but she could still write about beauty.

LAWRENCE: There is a long time for death. We should be involved with life. Death will take care of itself.

RHYS: Her husband, Murray. He wrote well of her in his diaries.

LAWRENCE: The book is a fraud by a poor writer. He will only stay alive because of his association with Katherine.

RHYS: I thought you knew him?

FRIEDA: We shared a cottage in Cornwall.

RHYS: It is always a shame to all out.

LAWRENCE: He tried to fuck his friends. (*Looks to FRIEDA.*)

RHYS is aghast. He recoils from the word and looks at FRIEDA and the other guests in the dining room. LAWRENCE is conscious of no difference.

FRIEDA: You must allow him his own turn of phrase, Mr Davies. It is fortunate the hotel is empty but it would make no difference.

LAWRENCE: You provoke me.

RHYS: I am not used to the colloquial translation.

LAWRENCE: I'll tell you about Murray. What he was really like. He tried to see Katherine when she was dying. A last chance at reconcilliation. You know what she screamed to the nurses? 'Keep the cunt away.' That's how much she loved him.

RHYS: You spoil some of my romantic illusions.

LAWRENCE: That's all they are. But then my wife knows him better than me.

FRIEDA: We all lived very close together. Perhaps too close.

LAWRENCE *(turns away from FRIEDA, is charming with RHYS)*: But tell me of your own. Is there anyone in the valley who waits for you?

RHYS: I... I kept to myself.

LAWRENCE: An observer.

RHYS: I had to be.

LAWRENCE: Because you're a writer?

RHYS: There was a dark lane where people went for a walk after chapel. They went in single and came out engaged. The thought of courting in an alley is too much for me.

LAWRENCE: So you are outside society looking in?

RHYS: It was more than that.

LAWRENCE: What then?

RHYS: I, I had certain considerations.

LAWRENCE: You are not without desire then?

RHYS: No, I...

LAWRENCE: The man in your book denies himself sex for too long. It suggests...

RHYS: I am not the man in my book.

LAWRENCE: But you identified with him?

RHYS: Yes, he denied himself things. I have done that. Now I am not sure I want to. I need to speak...

LAWRENCE: There is a brief time for sex and then a long time when it is out of place. You shouldn't miss the opportunity.

RHYS: I'm trying to... it's not always easy to say the things you want to with friends.

LAWRENCE: Come, it won't go further than us. And, when I put it in a book, the rest of the English speaking world.

142

RHYS: I'm trying to work things out... I'm...

FRIEDA: Lawrence, you ask too much of our young guest.

LAWRENCE: You think so? I wanted to know his inclinations.

FRIEDA: Not everyone shares your tastes in conversation. It is late.

LAWRENCE: Yes of course. I should be more civil. It is just that I am starved of conversation here. Intelligent conversation, and the first sign of it I see, I have to maul like a bear. Rhys, please forgive me, the excitement of your arrival has unexpectedly absorbed me. The long journey has tired me just thinking about it. I will retire, and bid you goodnight. (*With a final flourish, he retires, taking with him the last bottle of rosé.*)

FRIEDA: You mustn't be disturbed by him.

RHYS: He is an unusual man.

FRIEDA: You think so?

RHYS: Don't you?

FRIEDA: Of course, but I don't see him as others do. We are together. It is hard to see outside it.

RHYS: He is seen as someone who has gone his own way.

FRIEDA: Is that all?

RHYS: You misunderstand me.

FRIEDA: I think we all do that.

RHYS: For us younger writers – we read his words as if they are tablets inscribed in stone.

FRIEDA: You must tell him if that is so.

RHYS: I tried. He does not care.

FRIEDA: He feels so forgotten.

RHYS: Sightings of him are rare. He seems to take no part in the society of England.

FRIEDA: He is part of it but he hates it. What England is trying to do to his work. He writes only for others. Not for himself.

RHYS: He is not ignored.

FRIEDA: But he is censored. His work is not reaching his people. The people he writes the books for.

RHYS: Things will change.

FRIEDA: Yes, they must, but he may not live to see that.

RHYS: Surely he is a relatively young man. We must be optimistic for change.

FRIEDA: Maybe, but he is ill.

RHYS: He seems to struggle for breath.

FRIEDA: The bronchitis he complains about. He won't admit it.

RHYS: I see.

FRIEDA: He is well, now. But the attacks, they surround us, when they come they are terrible. I have to nurse him. It is not easy for a lover.

RHYS: I'm sure that there are difficulties.

FRIEDA: See, I am making you uncomfortable. Our new guest and already I pull you into lives you should know nothing about.

RHYS: It's not that. I'm just a little tired from the journey.

FRIEDA: All the way from Nice.

RHYS: I think I'd better retire.

FRIEDA: Then I will be eating alone.

RHYS: I'm sorry but I would like to wake early in the morning.

FRIEDA: You're planning on working while you're here?

RHYS: Yes, a little, I thought. It is a new place. I find I work well then.

FRIEDA: I shall see you at breakfast, then.

RHYS: Yes, good night.

FRIEDA: *Bon nuit.*

FRIEDA retreats. RHYS moves from the terrace, through the dining room, to the bedroom. He turns on the lamp and places his case on the bed. He begins unpacking, laying things out carefully, fussily, on the bed. He removes his dinner shirt and shoes. Then his trousers. He is dressed in silk underwear. As he moves his case from the bed, FRIEDA walks in. She wears a long dressing gown. RHYS reacts in surprise, verging on panic.

FRIEDA: I'm sorry, you obviously didn't hear my knock.

RHYS: No.

FRIEDA: It is no matter.

RHYS: I was just getting ready for bed.

FRIEDA: Yes, almost there.

RHYS scrambles to get a nightshirt from his case, then hurriedly puts it on.

FRIEDA: You feel the cold.

RHYS: This time of year.

FRIEDA: I find it easier to sleep with no clothes. They are too restricting, don't you feel?

RHYS: I... I'm not aware of it.

FRIEDA: No, perhaps not.

FRIEDA sits on the bed. RHYS looks for the door.

146

RHYS: Did you want anything?

FRIEDA: He is asleep.

RHYS: I can get you some lemonade.

FRIEDA: We have separate rooms.

RHYS: Shall I call the night porter?

FRIEDA: It is not good in a marriage to always sleep together.

RHYS: Shall I boil some water?

FRIEDA: I find coffee keeps me awake.

RHYS: Milk, then?

FRIEDA: Have you ever thought of getting married, Rhys?

RHYS: Er, not yet, no.

FRIEDA: You should consider it carefully.

RHYS: So I am told.

FRIEDA: I was married before Lawrence, you know.

RHYS: I was aware.

FRIEDA: I have been cruel to both men.

RHYS: I think it is part of our lives to be cruel to each other.

FRIEDA: Ernest, he loved me. And I him, as much as I could. I gave him my youth. He was a simple man. A fine, intelligent but simple man. I couldn't love him as I should have. It was Lawrence who saved me. He came to visit my husband but Ernest was at the Department so we took tea in the garden. The children where there, playing on the lawn. He was so direct. I'd met no one like that before. I couldn't stand the difference. He came again when my husband was there and again we spoke. I wanted to make love to him then, while my husband was in the house. He asked me quite directly to come away with him. He had nothing. No job, no money, prospects, nothing. I had no choice.

RHYS: It was a big sacrifice.

FRIEDA: I had to leave my children. They loved me, I was their world but if I had stayed I know I would have sacrificed my life for nothing. The children have grown without me, do you know how hard that has been? I have missed their childhood.

RHYS: Do you still see them?

FRIEDA: When we first returned to England I met them by chance, in Hyde Park. They were overjoyed to see me. They picked flowers from the park and thrust them into my hands. 'Mamma, you have come back to us.' They were laughing, running around with joy, that unbridled joy of children, my children. I cried then, really cried. But he wouldn't have it. He knew I had made my choice, 'You have chosen me' he said. 'The children will live without you, they will grow and be cared for. I need you.' Can you imagine a man who said that?

FRIEDA retreats into herself, on his bed. Short bursts of tears just break through. RHYS is unsure what to do but edges towards her and touches her shoulder. She doesn't look up. She sits on the bed. She begins to recover herself.

RHYS: He seems like a man who does need you.

FRIEDA: Yes, I loved him then. You do stupid, courageous things for love.

RHYS: I wouldn't know.

FRIEDA: There must have been someone for you, Rhys. A girl at home who broke your heart?

RHYS (*gets up from the bed, to give himself distance*): There was someone in London.

FRIEDA: Are you still in love?

LAWRENCE: It is gone now. There was a rushed marriage and I wasn't part of it.

FRIEDA: Where there children?

RHYS: Not as far as I know.

FRIEDA: What was she like?

RHYS: I didn't know her very well. (*He looks at FRIEDA, waiting for her reaction.*)

FRIEDA: I see. (*She smiles, wanting him to continue.*)

RHYS: Are you shocked?

FRIEDA: Rhys, of course not. Tell me about him.

RHYS: He was from Caerphilly.

FRIEDA: And you loved him?

RHYS: We had an arrangement.

FRIEDA: Did he love you?

RHYS: He was young, he was in the army, we had things in common. He would come back from exercise all fit, bursting. It was fun and he was gentle, really. We both knew it wouldn't last us long.

FRIEDA: And he left you?

RHYS: I think he had a better offer. Her father ran a haulage business in Croydon. I couldn't compete.

FRIEDA: Oh, Rhys. I'm sorry, but it's rather funny, no?

RHYS: I went to see his family, before I came away. They didn't hear from him much. His father thought I was rich and asked me for ten shillings so he could go drinking. They had no idea who I was. He could have mentioned me.

FRIEDA: What would he have said?

RHYS: That he had met someone? But no, we always have to hide it. This joy that we have so briefly. A sunny day in february. All light and hope and then it is gone.

They are both sat on the bed. They are relaxed, telling stories and being, perhaps, just friends.

FRIEDA: We are always forgetting our lovers. I try to picture some, my first husband and the only thing that returns is a blurred outline in his academic gown. Of his face – nothing.

RHYS: Some of mine wouldn't say hello to me in the street. They wouldn't recognise me in the street.

FRIEDA: But it is worth it, Rhys?

RHYS: I am not sure. I am driven by it.

FRIEDA: There is nothing wrong with sex. It is society that won't accept it.

RHYS: I think I need more than I am getting.

FRIEDA: We are all selfish in love. Lawrence is not. It is his generosity that allows me to live.

RHYS: He allows you...

FRIEDA: Freedoms. He knows I can only live with him. But there are other moments within life which we need. Experience is personal.

RHYS: But it is never as good as you think it will be.

FRIEDA: I'm not so sure. Maybe you're... (*she stops talking*) did you hear a cry?

RHYS (*stands up from the bed*): You must go. It is not proper if you were to be found here.

FRIEDA: He would presume. It is difficult now, when he is ill. He nurtured certain desires within me. I cannot now shut all that away. What is the use of all his work? We are a great experiment for him, his one dance with life. I am part of that.

It is him coughing. He will need me. I will see you at breakfast.

FRIEDA kisses RHYS, then leaves. RHYS is left agitated and unable to rest. He picks up a manuscript from his case and places it on the writing table. He cannot settle in to it. His nerves are on edge. He forces himself to sit.

The lights fade as RHYS works, then come up as the sun rises on the sea. RHYS has fallen asleep.

LAWRENCE settles at the breakfast table. He wears an African skull cap with beads. He has slept well and has a relaxed calm which surrounds him, as he opens his mail.

RHYS dresses and joins LAWRENCE at the table. RHYS is nervous and edges around LAWRENCE. Breakfast is served, on the table.

LAWRENCE: Sit down, man. I won't bite.

RHYS: I was unsure about what to order for breakfast.

LAWRENCE: *Pain*, *deux oeuf*, orange, coffee, *oui*? *C'est bon*.

RHYS: I had a late evening.

LAWRENCE: Yes, so did my wife. She is resting. She will not appear until lunch I expect.

RHYS: She is not ill?

LAWRENCE: *Tres mal*, as usual. It is the time of year or the month, I forget which.

RHYS: I see...

LAWRENCE: Don't mind the cap. It keeps my brain warm. My sister gave it to me. She bought it from an African. Did you have sisters?

RHYS: Yes, I still have them.

LAWRENCE: They are not with you?

RHYS: No.

LAWRENCE: Then sisters are always past tense because once you have lived with them being without them is never the same. You should know they have their moments.

RHYS: I still have some of the scars.

LAWRENCE: Tigers, were they?

RHYS: Once, but now they are so reserved.

LAWRENCE: The constraints of a chapel upbringing.

RHYS: I find them difficult to speak to. They conspire with my mother about matters I know nothing about.

LAWRENCE: Have they read your book?

RHYS: I have no idea. We do not discuss literature. I am perceived as a bit of an oddity.

LAWRENCE: It is not difficult to imagine, especially when you write.

RHYS: My mother still feeds me when I arrive home on the train with only the clothes I stand in.

LAWRENCE: Your finances are... irregular?

RHYS: On the back of the last novel, the drips have run together. Three gentlemen from Oxford have offered me an advance on a second. They said if I could at all afford it I should turn it down and write like a free man.

LAWRENCE: From the lips of someone who has an income of five hundred a year.

RHYS: You think I should take it?

LAWRENCE: Take the rings from their fingers. You will soon be on a battlefield for them.

RHYS: I need some more time to complete this book.

LAWRENCE: Then you should write them a letter accepting their generous offer.

RHYS: They might have forgotten by now.

LAWRENCE: They are Englishmen and they will honour their promises.

LAWRENCE: Are you working well?

RHYS: In the shuttered afternoons no one seems to do anything but sleep.

LAWRENCE: Or fuck.

RHYS: Yes, there is that.

LAWRENCE: I always found it a most convenient way to go to sleep.

RHYS: My landlady has a lover every Friday afternoon. They start at three, there is a break on the hour and finish at five. Never any variation.

LAWRENCE: The French have never been that imaginative.

RHYS: She has a husband.

LAWRENCE: They all do.

LAWRENCE returns his attention to his mail, but RHYS wants to talk.

RHYS: Is there an offer of advance in your mail?

LAWRENCE: No, but news of a plot to frustrate me further. The good lord provost the honourable Jix has found out where I am currently residing.

RHYS: Has the British Home Secretary power over here? In France?

LAWRENCE: No, none whatsoever, but he has the power to search all the mail coming into England. He's now employing people to open every piece of correspondence which pours out of Bandol.

RHYS: Everything?

LAWRENCE: Even the spinster who paints the flowers in the garden and is corresponding with her sister in Chichester. She is writing words to bring the English way of life to its knees.

RHYS: She might be excited?

LAWRENCE: Of course she'd be excited. Nothing else has ever happened in her life.

RHYS: How do you know about the post?

LAWRENCE: Our good friend Charlie Lahr has some contacts in the Home Office. He suspected that some of his mail had been tampered with. He asks a few questions and it is true.

RHYS: What will they do?

LAWRENCE: For now, nothing. Scotland Yard doesn't run the country and they shouldn't be allowed to.

RHYS: Will they arrest you?

LAWRENCE: Most probably.

RHYS: That's outrageous.

LAWRENCE: I feel as if I'm in the bloody war again. Bend over, Mr Lawrence, while we quickly check you haven't got anything hidden up there. Oh, yes, they have me alright, caged. I'm a prize exhibit for them. But let them put their fingers in the cage and I will bite and bite hard.

RHYS: There must be some protest we can make? Surely we are free men?

LAWRENCE: Yes, the men in the war thought they were dying for freedom. They gave it all up for an idea. An idea that already stinks in this England of fear and absurdity. But the words will outlast them. In fifty years time, no one will remember the honourable Jix – William Joynson Hicks, Home Secretary to king, country and empire. The only noteworthy thing he will have done in his life is try to read my mail. But they will still be reading the words he is trying to kill.

RHYS: We should do something?

LAWRENCE: Yes. There is always the balm of action.

RHYS: What?

LAWRENCE: When you return to Nice you can post some letters for me, from there. But for the books, I cannot do anything now.

RHYS: You mentioned another edition?

LAWRENCE: Yes it is possible, there are three drafts of *Lady Chatterley*. The first I wrote longhand. It is fine. There is nothing of the guts of the third but it could be published. What do you think?

RHYS: It may be a possibility.

LAWRENCE: You do not like it then?

RHYS: It is not that.

LAWRENCE: What then?

RHYS: *Sons and Lovers* is closer to my experience.

LAWRENCE: I cannot read it anymore. My mother comes alive again and talks to me and I was too hard on my father.

RHYS: You wrote his death a few times.

LAWRENCE: Then, I thought he deserved it.

RHYS: And now?

LAWRENCE: He was a good man but simple. Most of them are good and simple. They are sent under the ground at fourteen and never really see the light again. Tell me Rhys, I don't think you've seen that side of the life. How did you manage to escape it?

RHYS: I went undergroud.

LAWRENCE: Really?

RHYS: One sunday afternoon when it was closed. The pit foreman was a friend of my father's.

LAWRENCE: And your father's trade?

RHYS: He ran a book of bad debts and my mother ran a shop.

LAWRENCE: And the small world entered the shop?

RHYS: Yes, I believe it did. I was never forced to help. I did it because I wanted to. My mother had hopes of me getting an education but the walk to school was too far. I was bloody tired and usually wet by the time I arrived.

LAWRENCE: And so you escaped to London.

RHYS: Of sorts, but you exchange one prison for another. In London, I was thrown back on my world and with Charlie lending me books I found I could become a writer. One sunday afternoon I sat down and wrote three stories. They were as lean as winter sparrows. It was a start, I think.

LAWRENCE: Charlie must have liked them. Didn't they make it into the *Criterion*?

RHYS: No, not that, it was *The Coterie*. It didn't last long.

LAWRENCE: They never do on promises. But others spring up again like daisies. Every writer wants to edit a magazine. I've been trying for years.

RHYS: But you must reprint the book.

LAWRENCE: Yes, even if some quarters find it unpalatable.

RHYS: I've read of a new technique where you can makes copies from the original.

LAWRENCE: You must find out more.

RHYS: Perhaps in Paris, there's the bookshop Miss Beach runs.

LAWRENCE: Yes, the mad Englishwoman. She's had some success with publishing Joyce.

RHYS: And that's banned.

LAWRENCE: Heaven knows why.

RHYS: You don't like it?

LAWRENCE: He'll kill the novel, writing books like that.

RHYS: There's so much too it.

LAWRENCE: And it's all unreadable.

RHYS: I found Molly Bloom fascinating.

LAWRENCE: Joyce made her up. You can see his imagination and it has power, but... Joyce – that's all he really wants to tell you about, the world according to James Joyce. Joyce as he would really like to be. And he's too cerebral, all the fucking is in the head. Where's that going to get us?

RHYS: I'm not sure.

LAWRENCE: Rumour has it that he's started on another that he will publish in instalments until he is dead. God help us, please let it be quick.

RHYS: He must have a grand project in mind.

LAWRENCE: I'm sure he'll outlive me but it'll be such tedium. Him and that sprawling, stinking Irish family of his eating out at the best Parisian restaurants. He doesn't fucking pay for any of it. Joyce has an Englishman in one of his books claim that he always pays his way and then mocks him for it. That's the Irish Catholic for you. Wanting something for nothing. I always pay my way and I'm proud of it. Who else is going to do it?

RHYS: I prefer the Russians just now – Chekhov.

LAWRENCE: You look like a man who would fall for a Russian.

RHYS: I've tried.

LAWRENCE: He has heart but no muscle in his stories. They reach out to you but then leave you feeling short changed. Like a bad whore, you'd be better doing it yourself.

RHYS: I cannot agree.

LAWRENCE: No, you mustn't agree. Agreeing with me can be a disagreeable proposition. I fail to agree with myself regularly. It would be bad for my health if I did. I'd end up believing all sorts of the most outrageous nonsense.

FRIEDA enters.

LAWRENCE (*addressing FRIEDA*): Ah, here she is, a dreadnought on the high sea – only she'll last longer and cost more. I expect she'll want you to accompany her to the market or the church. She'll make a pretence of asking me to join you but it won't last long. She wants a young man to flirt with her. Do not disappoint her.

Yes, *fraulein*, we have breakfasted and dined without you. Do forgive Rhys's bad manners but someone kept him up late, last night. He claims it is his muse but I suspect a darker motive – would you like coffee?

FRIEDA: I was thinking of taking a late breakfast in the town.

LAWRENCE: As I said, extravagance.

FRIEDA: There is a café that serves excellent tarts. I thought we could all go.

RHYS: I'm afraid that I must work this morning.

LAWRENCE: Rhys, work in the afternoons, as you know. As a writer you face many challenges in life but the greatest is what to do with the afternoons.

FRIEDA: You will not accompany me?

LAWRENCE: No, I will not. I sleep in the afternoons.

FRIEDA: Philippe has offered to make the trap available for the day.

LAWRENCE: Then you mustn't ignore such a valuable offer.

FRIEDA: I cannot be seen alone with the proprietor of our hotel.

LAWRENCE: Then you will have to be seen with the unknown Mr Davies. Rhys will have to accompany you.

FRIEDA: It is only a short drive. To the church of Castellet. There is a wonderful fresco that you should see.

RHYS: I really should be getting on with some correspondence.

LAWRENCE: You have a lifetime for that. The duchess only has the trap for the morning. I will see if I can find you some bread from the kitchen. It would be a shame to rush back.... (*He gets up and walks into the hotel.*)

FRIEDA and RHYS are alone. They walk to the terrace. There is a sound of a trap and bells. The full light of the countryside surrounds them.

The sounds change from shoreline to a light wind through the cypresses.

FRIEDA is hot. RHYS is unsure. He has removed his jacket. His shirt is white. He opens the top button.

FRIEDA: The land here is so fertile.

RHYS: Yes, it is easier for life, I think. I heard a story that this is what is left after Creation. God took all his best bits and put them together to make Provence.

FRIEDA: And you believe these myths?

RHYS: I heard the same story about the Rhondda valley.

FRIEDA: Your faith is crumbling then?

RHYS: I take most of it as a story, now.

FRIEDA: Like love?

RHYS: I hope that is not a fiction. At present, I do not ask or expect much of people and therefore they will not let me down.

FRIEDA: You do not need to go through life closed to your world. It is not right. You need to be open to what the world can offer.

RHYS: I am finding more of that than I need.

FRIEDA: Do not close yourself to experience.

RHYS: Is that what marriage has taught you?

FRIEDA: When we first ran away together, everything was an adventure. To escape our world we walked over the mountains. I was a married woman of thirty with three children and I was walking through the mountains to Italy.

RHYS: I'm not a good walker.

FRIEDA: Neither am I but I am strong and there were many things I wanted to do. That he had opened my eyes to. When you are with him, everything comes alive again.

RHYS: He has a gift for seeing beauty.

FRIEDA: We had no money of course. I had always wanted to sleep in a hay loft. We slept in haylofts every night. They are cold, wind blows through the shutters and rain falls through the roof. By the time we reached Gargnano our clothes were in rags. It had taken five weeks. I was happy until I saw our reflection in an hotel window. We were tramps. Nothing but penniless vagrants.

RHYS: But you continued with him?

FRIEDA: By then I had no choice. He had forced me into it. My old life was in ruins. I couldn't admit it as a mistake. It was not a mistake.

RHYS: And your clothes?

FRIEDA: I booked into an hotel and refused to go out. I had to write to my sisters and beg for clothes and money just so I could go out again. Before Lawrence, I had never cooked. Never washed a bed sheet. I can cook macaroni now.

RHYS: It has been a trial then?

FRIEDA: The endless wandering? We have lived in so many houses that have not been my own. I need a home but he says the hotel is fine and comfortable. There is enough space to avoid each other as long as we have visitors.

RHYS: I'm sure he will find you a house. He mentioned Spain?

FRIEDA: Yes, there is always somewhere else to go. Another escape.

RHYS: Then you must press him. Tell him of your concerns.

FRIEDA: I cannot speak to him at all. He is not responding to me. I know it is the illness. He is scared of it.

RHYS: We are all scared of death a little, don't you think?

FRIEDA: It will come too early for him. He knows that. It is why he writes so much.

RHYS: The dry air will help his bronchitis.

FRIEDA: We have travelled the world looking for good air. It was not until Mexico that I knew he had consumption. I had been with him eight years then and he had not told me. It was the doctor there, in Spanish, he told me the truth as the blood poured from his lungs. It is terrible when they come, nothing is like it.

RHYS: A friend in the valley died a year after he had gone down the pit. He had no choice and he knew he was going to die but he still went. He would never admit it.

FRIEDA: They don't admit it to themselves. It is always bronchitis or a bad chest. That is good. A bad chest.

RHYS: There are things we need to keep to our souls.

FRIEDA: Have you ever made love to a woman, Rhys?

RHYS: I'm er...

FRIEDA: Is it too horrible to think about?

RHYS: My experience is in other areas.

FRIEDA: Do you know anything about their bodies?

RHYS: I had sisters and a maid from west Wales, we had to share a bed when we younger.

FRIEDA: But the real love of a woman? It does not interest you?

RHYS: I have my desires.

FRIEDA: Lawrence needs to live through a woman.

RHYS: I'm sure, he has his own way of doing things.

FRIEDA: He likes to take me like a dog takes a bitch.

RHYS: Ah, I see.

FRIEDA: Doesn't that interest you?

RHYS: There are some things that are best kept between lovers.

FRIEDA: You have no urge for the confessional?

RHYS: It has never helped me.

FRIEDA: Then you will never be a true writer.

RHYS: I will find enough truth.

FRIEDA: You need to experience it to write about it.

RHYS: I have a strong imagination.

FRIEDA: There is nothing like reality. It changes everything.

RHYS: I think we have to get back to the hotel.

FRIEDA: There is a pool in the rocks beyond the cypresses. I think we should bathe first. The water in the hotel is always salty.

RHYS: I have no towel or...

FRIEDA: Do you see the boys on the front with clothes on when they swim?

RHYS: Isn't February early to be swimming?

FRIEDA: For the French, yes. But I am a German. In the sunshine, we take our clothes off and burn.

FRIEDA disrobes. RHYS thinks about it, then removes his shirt. Pleased that she has won him, she moves forward and helps. There is excitement in her eyes as she pulls him, quickly, to the cypresses.

The light fades. There is a bell peal and laughter.

ACT TWO

At the hotel, LAWRENCE is sitting alone on the terrace. He is coughing and struggling with a letter. He folds it and leaves it on the table. He stands up and looks over the bay. He is agitated. He waits at the terrace staring, hostilely, out to sea. There is no sign of the trap. He stares malevolently at a passing waiter. He checks his pocket watch.

FRIEDA and RHYS climb the steps. They are jolly. RHYS is carrying his jacket, his shirt is worn loosely, with some buttons undone.

FRIEDA: Hello, a welcoming party of one.

LAWRENCE: It is gone four o'clock.

FRIEDA: Yes, so it is. The evening draws down on us.

LAWRENCE: What fucking manners you have woman. Show me some respect. I have been waiting here for two hours. Lunch is at one. You know well it is at one.

RHYS: You suggested we make the most of the day.

FRIEDA: And it has been such an excellent day. The sunshine.

LAWRENCE: I don't give a fuck for the sunshine, you whore.

FRIEDA: I think we must disagree.

LAWRENCE: I see a man I hardly know, two hours late accompanying my wife on some religious conversion of hers. (*Shouting:*) I have been sitting here for two hours.

RHYS: The frescoes were remarkable.

LAWRENCE: I bet they fucking were. Fat and German with great breasts that swing in the sunlight. I've seen them and they have been sucked dry by hungry mouths. Worn out with time and age.

FRIEDA: Lawrence, you are an uncouth pig.

LAWRENCE: And you are a shitbag.

RHYS: Please don't mind me.

FRIEDA: Ignore him, Mr Davies, the weather has changed, that is all.

LAWRENCE: Did he succour you last night.

RHYS: I really must object to this.

LAWRENCE: Well object then. Can you deny that she was in your room?

RHYS: We had a late conversation.

LAWRENCE: She calls it many things.

RHYS: I resent the accusation.

LAWRENCE: She is only disappointed you are not better looking. She would be happy then. But she's like a man – anything will do in the dark.

RHYS: The lights remained on. There was nothing untoward.

LAWRENCE: What would you know about it? Screwing your foreign boys with their tight, French arses in Nice.

RHYS: I cannot stand this any longer.

LAWRENCE: I expect you kneel for most of it.

RHYS: Excuse me. I think I will miss luncheon today. (*He walks past LAWRENCE.*)

LAWRENCE: You cannot. You cannot leave. I've ordered lobster.

RHYS: What?

LAWRENCE: It is a supplement on the menu.

RHYS: You want me to eat with you?

LAWRENCE: The chef has procured it especially. I have inspected them myself.

FRIEDA: Lawrence, what a kind man you are to our guest. (*She ruffles LAWRENCE's hair and kisses his cheek.*)

RHYS is standing in shock. FRIEDA and LAWRENCE move to the table. The blazing row has calmed them. RHYS has no idea if he is to join them, or flee.

LAWRENCE: Tell him, Frieda – it is ordered. He can't go to his room.

FRIEDA: Rhys, please join us. You cannot get lobster every day.

RHYS: I feel given the circumstances, I must. And I will be packing... (for the morning train).

LAWRENCE: Frieda, tell him. We have lobster.

FRIEDA (*moves back to RHYS*): My husband has obviously laid plans for us, Rhys. It would be best for us all if you can join us.

RHYS consents; moves unsurely, towards the dining table.

FRIEDA: You cannot let a little disagreement spoil a good lobster.

Lights fade. Time passes.

RHYS moves to his room. LAWRENCE and FRIEDA exit. RHYS begins to pack. He puts on his tie. FRIEDA enters, dressed in bright colours.

RHYS: I was preparing to leave...

FRIEDA: Yes, I can see.

RHYS: I considered it would be easier.

FRIEDA: No, it wouldn't be that.

RHYS: I don't know how you put up with him.

FRIEDA: The fishermen came in early today. They say there is a storm coming down from the mountains. It won't be a good day to travel.

RHYS: I'm not going by boat.

FRIEDA: You have to leave at a propitious time.

RHYS: He swore at you again.

FRIEDA: He always swears at me.

RHYS: In public.

FRIEDA: We have to. There is nowhere else.

RHYS: It is a terrible way to treat a lady.

FRIEDA: Oh, that wasn't terrible. You haven't seen us when we are terrible together. You must have heard the stories? How he beats me with a willow rod?

RHYS: I never believed them.

FRIEDA: And now you do?

RHYS: I have never heard a man swear at a woman.

FRIEDA: Oh, Rhys, that is nothing. We have so many battles to fight out. So much to get rid of. We are both good fighters.

RHYS: I think I would leave.

FRIEDA: What for? I would only have to come back.

RHYS: He frightens me with his rages for you.

FRIEDA: He's a genius.

RHYS: That excuses nothing.

FRIEDA: There is nothing like living with a creative man. I didn't want a calm sea.

RHYS: He pours all his anger into you.

FRIEDA: With great anger there is a great love. Sometimes I hate him like the devil himself. But I can take him like the weather. Here is a spring day, glorious sunshine. Then another day – alas all has changed, it is chilly and it rains and I wish, how I wish it were sunny again.

RHYS: I cannot see it.

FRIEDA: He has to treat us this way. You must try to understand him.

RHYS: Two weeks of him is enough for a lifetime.

FRIEDA: Don't say that. He needs us now.

RHYS: Last week I was his great new friend and now I am the devil.

FRIEDA: You are a fine friend. A friend we have found here.

RHYS: Does he always hate his friends?

FRIEDA: You must not let his words stay with you.

RHYS: I am a writer. I listen and record. He knows that as well as anyone.

FRIEDA: He is in need of you now.

RHYS: My mind is made up.

FRIEDA: We both need you.

RHYS: Why?

FRIEDA: Can't you see?

RHYS: I see I was invited for ridicule.

FRIEDA: No.

RHYS: What then? A prize exhibit?

FRIEDA: It is hard for me. To live with him alone. There are no others in this place who even begin to understand him. All they see is this monster.

RHYS: The beast of Bandol.

FRIEDA: Yes, if you like. He's in this cage but they can't tame him.

RHYS: And what am I to do?

FRIEDA: You help us live a little. Even our quarrels are old now.

RHYS: So I am an audience?

FRIEDA: You misunderstand me. I am tired of this constant moving, always on the edge of the world.

RHYS: Is that your world, him?

FRIEDA (*turns away*): Am I the stupid German *milchcow*? The woman who the English think have ruined him?

RHYS: No, I'm sorry, I didn't mean it like that.

FRIEDA: Yes you did. I'll always just be his wife. The woman who gave up everything to be part of a man of genius. I could see it in him and I took my chance with history.

RHYS: Hardly a romance.

FRIEDA: Rhys, don't be cruel to me. He was a good writer when I met him. He is a great writer now. Do you think I had nothing in that?

RHYS: I can see you release things in him.

FRIEDA: I loved him. He moved things in me. I wasn't living before, just sleepwalking. He changed the world for me.

RHYS: And now all things are the same?

FRIEDA: You don't understand. I am part of this life he has made. His work, without me, would have faded. Don't you see that?

RHYS: He'd written books before you met.

FRIEDA: Only one. Unpublished, unknown, unrecognised. The women in his books, the ones who matter – they are all me and my sisters.... He has used my life, our life together, to create his art.

RHYS: And is it worth it, for you? To be treated so disgracefully... to become art.

FRIEDA: I have no choice, Rhys. And you would know if you had been in love with a woman.

RHYS: That wouldn't be easy.

FRIEDA: Sorry, that was me being unfair.

RHYS: So what? I asked for it. It's just part of your games. Even I have to take part.

FRIEDA: I need you here just now, Rhys.

RHYS: So you can recover your love?

FRIEDA: I have not lost it.

RHYS: You came into my bedroom, naked.

FRIEDA: What is a little intimacy between friends?

RHYS: I cannot respond to you.

FRIEDA: You are a man.

RHYS: We are not all enslaved to our cocks.

FRIEDA: We are beings of sexuality. It is a spectrum. That is what his books are about.

RHYS: Do we always have to return to his bloody books?

FRIEDA: Sex is a gift. It controls us.

RHYS: It is an unwanted present from an old maiden aunt.

FRIEDA: You have to spend what you have.

RHYS: I do.

FRIEDA: When?

RHYS: There are opportunities. In Nice, there are places.

FRIEDA: So you frequent the brothels like any other high-born Englishman.

RHYS: I don't usually have to pay.

FRIEDA: We all have different prices.

RHYS: I am not cheap.

FRIEDA: He warned me you would not like me.

RHYS: You know that is not the case.

FRIEDA: He sensed it in you.

RHYS: He is a man of perceptions. All this machismo. It fools no one. He is afraid of himself. He has to hide it behind something else.

FRIEDA: I think you have misunderstood him.

RHYS: I take what I see.

FRIEDA: Hah, a pool of mirrors. His depths reflect your desires.

RHYS: I am not attracted to sick, old men.

FRIEDA: Don't force your anger on to us. You are too young for it.

RHYS: You need more of me than I can give.

FRIEDA: We are creatures of our senses, Rhys. It was fun in the pool. Let me touch you like that again.

RHYS: Doesn't it hurt you to betray him?

FRIEDA: Free love is no betrayal. He understands me.

RHYS: I have my reservations.

FRIEDA: Are you without desire or curiosity?

RHYS: Can we get away from sex?

FRIEDA: I can't see how you can do that? The bars you frequent on the Nice harbour. Aren't they filled with old men?

RHYS: Not all of them.

FRIEDA: Do you think you'll be able to live as openly in England?

RHYS: I find Bloomsbury very forgiving.

FRIEDA: They'll fuck anyone there.

RHYS: I can be discreet as you are not.

FRIEDA: I don't need to be. He is understanding of my needs.

RHYS: Is that why he invited me here? Dear Mr Davies, would you care to spend a few days with my wife?

FRIEDA: He is not my pimp.

RHYS: I'm sorry. I have been here two weeks. It has been both terrible and beautiful. You both have an honesty and a passion which is too much for me.

FRIEDA: You could go away for a few days and then return. Perhaps post his poems back to England. He would like that. Please don't just leave us, Rhys.

RHYS: I could do that.

FRIEDA: There is love here for us all, Rhys.

FRIEDA moves forward and puts her arms around RHYS. She kisses him, lightly, like a mother might.

The lights fade on the bedroom.

RHYS leaves. Time passes. LAWRENCE appears on the terrace. FRIEDA goes to him and helps him dress against the cold that now threatens them. There is a ritual beauty to it. His cough has deepened. FRIEDA leaves, briefly. She returns carrying several letters and a parcel, which she places on the table.

LAWRENCE: This bloody cold wind, I've had enough of it.

FRIEDA: It'll pass.

LAWRENCE: When?

FRIEDA: The mistral only lasts a few days.

LAWRENCE: It's been blowing for a week.

FRIEDA: There's snow on the mountains. Once the snow melts, the wind will cease.

LAWRENCE: That could be months.

FRIEDA: The mountain air will be good for your bronchials.

LAWRENCE: It has killed the palm trees. Have you seen them? They are frozen.

FRIEDA: They will come back with the spring.

LAWRENCE: How can they do that? They're dead.

FRIEDA: Surely not.

LAWRENCE: We will have to go to Spain.

FRIEDA: It's too far.

LAWRENCE: We'll go by boat. To Majorca.

FRIEDA: I want to see mother.

LAWRENCE: Hell to your bloody family.

FRIEDA: You need rest, not travel.

LAWRENCE: That's what the doctors tell me. Are you a doctor too?

FRIEDA: Rhys is coming to see us again. I think there's a parcel from him on the table.

LAWRENCE: He hasn't forgotten us then? (*Walks to the table and picks up the parcel.*)

FRIEDA: He is such a sweet boy.

LAWRENCE: Pity he's the wrong sex.

FRIEDA: He has enough passion to survive.

LAWRENCE: I felt he will always be an outsider. It will tire him in the end.

FRIEDA: And me.

LAWRENCE: Look, he has sent me silk pyjamas. What in the earth for?

FRIEDA: Because he saw the filthy rags you have taken to wearing.

LAWRENCE: There's such thing as bad taste.

FRIEDA: They're the very thing for the young and rich on the blue coast.

LAWRENCE: And I am neither. Do you think he is trying to tell me something?

FRIEDA: You always suspect the most base motives.

LAWRENCE: He intrigues me. It will be good to see him again. He needs a bit more of my influence.

FRIEDA: He is already drunk with it. I finally read his book.

LAWRENCE: It wasn't that bad.

FRIEDA: He might as well have titled it After D H Lawrence.

LAWRENCE: He has good taste in reading.

FRIEDA: And the sex was all repressed and guilty.

LAWRENCE: He's Welsh.

FRIEDA: You are the high priest of liberation. So much for your influence.

LAWRENCE: As a disciple he lacks discipline.

FRIEDA: I hope his second is better.

LAWRENCE: I fear it is worse.

FRIEDA: Another book about the mining districts. You've done all that to death.

LAWRENCE: I suggested he find his Celtic mysticism. I'm afraid he thought I was serious. He'll end up writing like that Irish clown, Joyce.

FRIEDA: He's too timid for a great book.

LAWRENCE: Great books can only be written by great men.

FRIEDA: Without a woman he will come to nothing.

LAWRENCE: How can he possibly have a woman?

FRIEDA: He might change.

LAWRENCE: I'm sure you'll make yourself available if he does.

FRIEDA: I think he is lost now.

LAWRENCE: Of course he is. What else would he be doing in the south of France. The place is crammed with people lost. Even we are bloody lost. I had a letter from Wells yesterday. He wants me to say a few words for his new journal. A message to the common man. Why do they all think I know the common man? I never went down the bloody pit. Write something for the people, they say. The people don't want to bloody hear it. I'll give them something. Yes, we need a revolution, but of life. Not in the name of money or work. Smash money. What we want is life and trust. Men trusting men, making living a free thing. Not a thing to be earned.

FRIEDA: Maybe they don't want freedom. The lower classes need education and instruction, not freedom.

LAWRENCE: Spoken by a woman who couldn't cook macaroni when she first fucked a common man.

FRIEDA: Why do you always bring it back to us?

LAWRENCE: Because I am a married man. There is no one else but us.

FRIEDA: Does Rhys think he will be able to travel to Paris with you?

LAWRENCE: Says he will. He'll stay for a few days and then we will depart. I've had enough of this accursed place.

FRIEDA: Write back to him, immediately. I can leave you with him at Lyon. I will travel on to see my mother at Baden.

LAWRENCE: Lyon – no – we'll go on the day train.

FRIEDA: You'll take two days to reach Paris.

LAWRENCE: So what? We'll take a hotel. It'll be fun.

FRIEDA: It'll be slow.

LAWRENCE: I'll go in a wheel barrow if I can get someone to push it.

FRIEDA: I wonder if Rhys is used to such speeds.

LAWRENCE: He will be fine. Do you think Paris is safe?

FRIEDA: The air should be clearing there now.

LAWRENCE: I don't like it but I must get an edition of *Lady Chatterley* printed. Wells tells me they are on sale on the Left Bank for twelve guineas.

FRIEDA: Rhys will make a good travel companion, I think.

LAWRENCE: He is as poor as we were. I expect I'll have to meet the bill.

FRIEDA: He will pay his way as you have done. You must let him do it.

LAWRENCE: He is penniless and sending me silk pjamas. I will scold him about it as soon as he arrives.

FRIEDA strips the bed. She removes some of the effects of Bandol, then leaves.

The train arrives. RHYS is dressed for travel. LAWRENCE joins him. They make the journey north. Paris has a different sound and smell.

RHYS heaves Lawrence's case on to the bed. LAWRENCE sits on the bed, beside the case. He is exhausted – the journey has worn him out and his cough is harsher and deeper.

LAWRENCE: Did you see the man?

RHYS: I couldn't avoid him.

LAWRENCE: I thought he was a fool.

RHYS: He was lost in the city.

LAWRENCE: And then his eyes. I could not be angry with a man who had such eyes. He was a man who lived truly in his blood, not in his head.

RHYS: He will find the city cold towards him.

LAWRENCE: Yes, it cannot be avoided.

RHYS: This is his escape.

LAWRENCE: Why do they come here? To be despised by the French? They are such a despicable nation. They are charging us far too much for these rooms. The centre of Paris. I hate it as much as I hate London and I will never go back there. I always felt done for if the train was heading to London.

RHYS: I find London insulates me. I'm not sure I could live anywhere else now.

LAWRENCE: Then I think you are trapped for life.

RHYS: There are so many people and no one knows my name.

LAWRENCE: That is not good for sales.

RHYS: I plan to go to Brighton regularly.

LAWRENCE: You will come through. But I'd prefer not to look.

RHYS: It's a nice place by the sea.

LAWRENCE coughs heavily, unable to hold his breath. He is struggling for breath, composure. He is trying to keep calm, but through the coughing, a storm grows. His illness in the city is gaining on him.

RHYS: Shall I call for a drink?

LAWRENCE: No, I will be alright.

RHYS: Was the meeting a success?

LAWRENCE: He is not the man I would have chosen has a publisher but I am a beggar in this city, now.

RHYS: I think Miss Beach should have done it.

LAWRENCE: She's obsessed with Joyce. It will probably be the only book she will ever publish.

RHYS: The new man, is he American?

LAWRENCE: I think so, he offered to do a uniform edition.

RHYS: Of all the books?

LAWRENCE: Eventually. The Peagasus Press. Sounds unlikely to me.

RHYS: It would be a fine set.

LAWRENCE: He kept offering me money. Insisting he had a cheque in his pocket and he could write it out for me now. Nine hundred dollars. As if I was going to kick his fat, American arse for it. They're despicable, expect you to fawn on their stinking money. He's only offering me money because it will make more for him. My words have value. Not the man I would have chosen. If only the English publishers had balls. But no, they run from my fires.

RHYS: When do you think the new edition could be ready by?

LAWRENCE (*calmer, checking his papers*): He promises me he will work quick. A few weeks at most.

RHYS: I could take a few copies back to England in my suitcase?

LAWRENCE: Yes, you must do that. It will be very helpful.

RHYS: I know a few friends who will buy copies.

LAWRENCE: Tell them they will be making a sound investment in the education of their children.

RHYS: I'm not sure many of them will have children.

LAWRENCE: No, it is a shame for a man not to have children. The course of life has been damned.

RHYS: I wouldn't be able to cope.

LAWRENCE: You have to.

RHYS: You have none yourself.

LAWRENCE: I tried hard enough.

RHYS: Frieda has her family.

LAWRENCE: Yes, and she has had me. But children, they are what we live for. Nothing else is worth a damn. I thought they would come. I wanted them, but no.

RHYS: Your health would have suffered.

LAWRENCE: Then let it suffer.

Beat.

LAWRENCE slides into another bout of coughing.

LAWRENCE: There's nothing bloody wrong with my health a good doctor couldn't cure.

RHYS: Then we must send for one.

LAWRENCE: There aren't any.

RHYS: I don't think I will ever have children.

LAWRENCE: Then we are the same for different reasons.

RHYS: I found my younger brother a creature who had nothing to do with me.

LAWRENCE: They are so noisy and they won't keep still. And of course they can't keep still because they are so happy, really happy before it is all beaten out of them and they enter the world of us adults and fuck it up all over again.

RHYS: What of Frieda?

LAWRENCE: She wanted them with me, sure enough. They wouldn't come and we had to find another way into the future.

RHYS: I feel like there is no need for them.

LAWRENCE: Love in itself may be enough for you. It has had to be for me.

RHYS: You don't despise me for it? For needing something different?

LAWRENCE: Of course not. As long as there is no compulsion or force, there is no hurt. It is the same in all things.

RHYS: I find people always hurt each other.

LAWRENCE: Yes, it is the way.

RHYS: It fills me with lust and fear.

LAWRENCE: There is always surrender in being fucked. You have to be passive. Like a slave. It is an assertion of power. It asks a lot to be taken that way. There is a darkness, an animal within us, but it is part of life. No one speaks about it. Men want it and women find a release in it. A burning out of shames, the deepest, oldest shames in the secret places. Oh Celia, Celia shits.

RHYS: I can't do it. I am afraid of it.

LAWRENCE: There is a flame to it that will consume you. As long as there is no harm or force.

RHYS: Will it free me from the guilt?

LAWRENCE: Freedom is about pleasure, pain – it doesn't matter. Life knows its own. (*He breaks down into another coughing fit.*)

RHYS: Mr Lawrence, please. I will fetch a doctor.

LAWRENCE: I shouldn't have left Bandol. It made me feel so much better.

RHYS: It was a... decent place.

LAWRENCE: And you, Mr Davies? I suspect your time in the south is finished?

RHYS: I shall be returning to London. For the season.

LAWRENCE: What have you bought with your time?

RHYS: Nice has tired me with it's demands. Life – but nothing else.

LAWRENCE: No happiness?

RHYS: I have learnt not to expect it and I am never disappointed.

LAWRENCE: And thou shall not receive.

RHYS: I think I just wanted some peace.

LAWRENCE: Shame on you that you ask for peace. I don't want peace. I go around the world fighting.

RHYS: Is there no end to it?

LAWRENCE: You can succumb to life or fight it. Life is a great procession but it keeps marching in the right direction. Impersonal but not without purpose.

RHYS: But then why have I been like I am? I have found nothing with my life, nothing.

LAWRENCE: Then you are not fighting hard enough.

RHYS: But why is it given to me to fight for anything?

LAWRENCE: You were different, that is all.

RHYS: Have you found it, then? All this scuttling from one place to another?

LAWRENCE: In the grave I find my peace. First let me fight and win through. (*He cascades into another fit.*)

RHYS: I must fetch someone.

LAWRENCE: No, no one. I hate doctors. They would have ruined me. I am not going to die in a Paris hotel room. I will not. They are waiting for me. The fucking vultures. They have been circling since I escaped them in London. They want me to die so they can put me in their fucking memoirs and diaries. It is the only thing that will ever live after them – their association with me. They could do it now but they are cowards. They know if they write about me, I will write back and put them in a book and it will be better and harsher and truer than anything they can do. I will have them for my betrayal, this bloody England who has tried to drown me. It can drown. Cover it with waves and let the water rush over it all. They have hated me with their titles and their money. I was the monkey. The miner's son who had come out of the earth. I fitted all their theories of advancement with conditions. And when I made fun of them they hated me even more. My England. It stinks.

LAWRENCE breaks into a violent rage with his coughing. Blood smears over RHYS's shirt as he tries to soothe him. LAWRENCE is having a haemorrhage.

RHYS: What can I do?

LAWRENCE: Nothing.

RHYS continues to hold LAWRENCE.

LAWRENCE: Morphia, get some. In my case.

RHYS gives LAWRENCE a bottle from the case. It soothes him of his coughing. Gradually, he falls asleep in RHYS's arms. RHYS retires to a chair and waits, as dawn comes up over Paris. FRIEDA enters.

FRIEDA: I came as soon as I could.

RHYS: He has not had a good night.

FRIEDA: Was there blood?

RHYS: Some. He asked for the morphia. It was eased then.

FRIEDA: Is he sleeping now?

RHYS: Yes, I think so.

FRIEDA: You have been good to us, Rhys.

RHYS: I'm just trying to help. We all owe him a lot.

FRIEDA: It has helped him... to have a man to talk to.

RHYS: I will try to be honest about him.

FRIEDA: I'm sure you will. There are enough snakes in our lives. There will be traitors enough when he can't defend himself. But I will defend him. I have enough resources.

RHYS: He has done enough for you?

FRIEDA: It has been hard, really. In every way imaginable. But once, when we were high up in the mountains, he told me then that he loved me. Nothing has mattered but you. Nothing at all. Without me it would not have been worth it. They are cruel to us, Rhys, they don't understand. They hate it that I am German and they hate it that I am part of him. He is one of the greatest men and they want to keep him English. This charade we have played. It has gone on and we can't run forever.

RHYS: Will he have treatment?

FRIEDA: He knows he is dying. The doctor in Mexico gave him two years to live – that was six years ago. He can rise from this again. He is an artist, not like other men. It is just force of will that is keeping him alive. If he had stayed in England he would have died years ago. He would have been a minor poet. That is all. I am in the books as I was in life. They will see it in the end. When all of us are dead and forgotten. But they can't forget him. His work has changed things for us. They do not see it yet.

RHYS withdraws from the bedroom.

FRIEDA enters the room. She uncovers the bedclothes. LAWRENCE is exposed. She removes his blood-stained shirt. She washes his face with a flannel. She lays him out, ceremonially, on the bed. She fetches a clean shirt, a jacket and beret. She kisses him and he allows her to dress him. As the lights of Paris close around them, she kisses him for the last time, like a mother.

RHYS is waiting for time to pass. He ventures south for a lifetime. His life passes before him. The ghosts of his past swirl. The focus is of a warm shoreline. Waiting. He is on the front at the Beau Rivage. The sun has come up on the Mediterranean. He takes off his shoes and socks and bathes his feet in the water. The light surrounds.

From a distance, a man can be heard whistling – LAWRENCE, restored to life in this place where they wait by the shore. He enters.

LAWRENCE: So you are waiting for me, I hear, Mr Davies.

RHYS: I'm so glad you could come.

LAWRENCE: *Bon journaie*, as they say, for you?

RHYS: I am a little tired.

LAWRENCE: You have not come far.

RHYS: I couldn't get out of London.

LAWRENCE: It can hold you too tight. I tended to avoid cities if I could. I always felt done for if the train was heading to London.

RHYS: It held my life. With a few excursions.... I went to Brighton regularly.

LAWRENCE: It's a nice place by the sea.

Beat.

LAWRENCE: I like this place. It makes me feel so much better. I should have expected that. Did you keep working?

RHYS nods.

LAWRENCE: Did it bring you anything?

RHYS: A life.

LAWRENCE: But no happiness?

RHYS: I didn't expect it and I wasn't disappointed. Thou shallt not receive.

LAWRENCE: You should have had children. Wanting them was the thing that kept me alive. You either have to succumb to this life or fight it.

RHYS: I think I just wanted peace.

LAWRENCE: Shame on you that you ask for peace.

RHYS: Is there no end to it? I have found nothing with my life, nothing. I have covered myself all the way.

LAWRENCE: Then you did not fight hard enough.

RHYS: I was not made for fighting.

LAWRENCE: You were different that's all.

Beat.

RHYS: They still talk about you.

LAWRENCE: So I hear. But I never read reviews. And you, did you make your mark?

RHYS: A few scratches.

LAWRENCE: I told you to put more sex in your work.

RHYS: I wanted to explain the power. That they are stronger than us.

LAWRENCE: Of course, but there is no power without sex.

RHYS: Then I must defer to you.

LAWRENCE: Still, this isn't such a bad place to end up.

Beat.

LAWRENCE: There was a young man at the hotel asking about you.

RHYS: I know.

LAWRENCE: He's Welsh, I hear. Writing about you and me. Imagine that.

RHYS: I do find I always attract the most unsuitable people. It comes with having money.

LAWRENCE: How did you become rich? Surely not by writing?

RHYS: People kept dying on me. It was most conveinent.

LAWRENCE: Still, he's worth a look. I hear he's doing his best.

RHYS: *I hear* his French is terrible.

LAWRENCE: Don't let the language bother you.

RHYS: I'm not sure he's my type.

LAWRENCE: Still choosy. You should have been more like Frieda. She would have cured you.

RHYS: Please give her my regards.

LAWRENCE: She is happy, you know. I always made her happy. I was a married man at heart. (*He leaves.*)

RHYS picks up a few stones from the shore and skims them out to sea. The south closes in.

LEWIS DAVIES

Lewis Davies is a novelist, short-story writer, publisher and playwright.

Amongst his plays are *Without Leave* (1998), *My Piece of Happiness* (1998), *Sex and Power at the Beau Rivage* (2003), *Football* (2004), and *Spinning the Round Table* (2005).

His travel book *Freeways, A Journey West on Route 66* won the 1994 John Morgan Award and in 1999 he won the Rhys Davies Prize for *Mr Rooprantna's Chocolate*.

His novels include *Work, Sex and Rugby* (1993), *Tree of Crows* (1996), and *My Piece of Happiness* (2000).

As I was a Boy Fishing – a collection of essays, vignettes and poems – was published in 2003. He edited an edition of Welsh fiction entitled *Urban Welsh*.

A GUEST AT THE BEAU RIVAGE

Rhys Davies

Nice, winter, 1928. A young writer flushed with the success of his first novel is sitting struggling with a second. In the calm of a shuttered afternoon a letter is pushed under his door. It is an invitation from the most talked about man of his time. An invitation. "Would you care to come here and be my guest in this small and inexpensive hotel for a few days? Bandol is on the Marseilles side of Toulon. My wife and I would both be pleased if you come." And with the letter Rhys Davies caught the train to Bandol to meet D H Lawrence and a place in literary history.

Lawrence in 1928 had reached a final synthesis of his talents with the private publication in Italy of *Lady Chatterley's Lover*. It had yet to reach the notoriety of later years but copies were being seized at customs in America and England. To Rhys he had appeared 'a remote, inaccessible figure, brooding and isolated... a kind of John the Baptist in the Wilderness.'

Lawrence met him at the station. Rhys was taken by how relaxed and un-English he seemed. Frieda was also there and they were both pleased to see him.

Rhys had been invited out of interest, they shared a mining background, and out of the desire of an older writer to help a younger. He was also there to bolster the Lawrence's long marriage. They had always needed people around them to take some of the heat from a relationship that was often brutal and wonderful at the same time.

He would not escape some of the rages of Lawrence against youth, England and the world. 'All you young writers have me to thank for what freedom you enjoy, even as things are – for being able to say much that you couldn't even hint at before I appeared. It was I who set about smashing down barriers.'

But Rhys was charmed. Lawrence took an interest in his work and helped him revise some of his stories and warned him not to worry about his novel. It would come. Frieda also liked him and he accompanied her on long walks around the bay at Bandol.

After Paris, Rhys returned to London and kept in touch with the Lawrences through letter. For Rhys his brush with Lawrence was an important moment in what was to be a long literary career. He wrote ten novels and several collections of short stories in 50 years of work. His work was published worldwide and attracted praise from writers such as Graham Greene and John Betjeman. He was awarded the OBE for services to literature in 1968. His novels have faded from view. His work largely forgotten. It is only recently, through the Rhys Davies Trust set up through the generosity of his brother, that a popular and critical reappraisal of his work has begun. His short stories have reappeared in print, their tight structures, still as lean as winter sparrows, reveal a writer who revelled in the description of the human condition.

Lewis Davies

The Human Condition: Selected Short Stories of Rhys Davies
(£5.99 Parthian).

(First published in *A470* magazine, 2003.)

PARTHIAN

diverse probing
profound **urban**
epic **comic**
rural savage
new
writing

www.parthianbooks.co.uk

LIBRARY OF WALES

www.libraryofwales.org

Independent
Presses
Management

www.inpressbooks.co.uk

Llyfrau ar-lein
Books on-line